A Father's Memories

A Father's Memories

Makoto Shiina

Translated by
Frederik L. Schodt

KODANSHA INTERNATIONAL
Tokyo ▪ New York ▪ London

Illustrations by Hitoshi Sawano

Distributed in the United States by Kodansha America, Inc.,
114 Fifth Avenue, New York, New York 10011, and in the
United Kingdom and continental Europe by Kodansha
Europe, Ltd., Gillingham House, 38-44 Gillingham Street,
London SW1 1HU.
Published by Kodansha International, Ltd., 17-14 Otowa 1-
chome, Bunkyo-ku, Tokyo 112, and Kodansha America, Inc.

First Edition 1992
92 93 94 10 9 8 7 6 5 4 3 2 1
ISBN 4-7700-1693-X

Library of Congress Cataloging-in-Publication Data

Shiina, Makoto, 1944-
[Gaku monogatari. English]
My Boy: A Father's Memories / Shiina Makoto.
p. cm.
ISBN 4-7700-1693-x
I. Title.
PL861.H4968G3513   1993
895.6 ' 35--dc2
92-23377 CIP

CONTENTS

My Boy

A Father's Memories

Fragrant Olive

My son's name is Gaku. When he started preschool, my wife and I told him we had named him with the second *kanji* character of the Japanese word for mountains, *san-gaku*, because we both liked mountain climbing. He gave a brief nod and replied with a bored expression, "Oh, really?"

My wife was herself teaching preschool then, and she had to leave the house very early in the morning—by seven, in fact. Since I worked at home, writing essays on everything and anything for next to nothing, the job of escorting Gaku to and from his school fell to me. As I soon learned, at his age preschool is the dominating experience in life, and to enter it is to enter an enchanted, thrill-packed world where parents' voices no longer register.

One day, a family from a nearby town moved into our neighborhood, and a little tyke with the traditional sounding name of

Kenjiro Yoshikawa became one of Gaku's classmates. Soon Kenjiro began coming over to play at our house nearly every day after school, accompanied by his one-year-older, first-grade brother, Noboru. All three boys, including my son, had shaved heads, and when they were walking together they looked like a cartoon drawing of young Buddhist monks.

Kenjiro and Noboru lived with their mother, who had apparently been divorced several years earlier. One day I was peeling a *nashi* pear for the boys after school when Noboru, the first grader, suddenly announced with an angry look, "My daddy died and went to Hell." I assumed that was the way his mother explained his father's absence to him, but I was shocked by the intense hatred it seemed she harbored.

The mother was employed at a pharmaceutical firm in the Tokyo area, and although I don't know what sort of work she did, she left home at different times on different days. When I took Gaku to school at eight-thirty in the morning, I began running into her. She was striking—slender, petite, with well-defined features.

We first met on the path that led through a little wood to the preschool. Gaku and her son Kenjiro immediately began frolicking like friendly dogs, which left the two of us walking together through the wood in silence, wheeling our bicycles and feeling awkward. The autumn breeze was increasingly nippy.

"You've been awfully kind to my children," she said, bowing deeply and adding, "I can't thank you enough." Then, just before the path through the woods emerged onto a paved road, she suddenly exclaimed in a bright voice, "The children told me you treated them to a wonderful bowl of *soba* noodles the other day."

At first I was so surprised I couldn't remember doing so.

"I did?" I said.

"The children said Gaku's father made them some delicious

cold noodles with fried tofu. Now they keep begging me to make some, too."

I suddenly realized what she was talking about. "Oh, *that*," I said, laughing despite myself. A little while before, on a whim, I had thrown together some fried tofu, thinly sliced green onions, shreds of dried bonito, and soy sauce, and improvised a cold soba dish for the kids. I had had absolutely no idea what it would taste like, but it had turned out surprisingly good, so with a straight face I had bragged to them that, "Only three of the most famous chefs in Japan know how to make cold *soba* noodles this fantastic."

In the continuing breeze, Kenjiro's mother turned to me and said seriously, "I'd really appreciate it if you could show me how to make those noodles sometime."

"I, uh, er, well, it's not easy," I stammered in reply. I hurriedly parked my bike where the path ended, turned back to Gaku and Kenjiro, who were still dashing around the wood like dogs, and yelled, "Over here on the double, boys!"

When we emerged from the wood the wind picked up, and it carried with it a whiff of perfume from Kenjiro's mother. As befitted the season, she was wearing the scent of fragrant olive.

The shaved-head gang of three gathered at our house every day after school, to play furiously. While I worked upstairs, I could often hear their shrill voices echoing from the yard and the street in front.

One day their voices suddenly fell silent, and from the corner of the yard I heard an odd sound of running water. It seemed to go on for ever. Suspicious, I glanced out the window and saw to my horror that the entire yard was covered in brown mud. The boys were covered in it, too, and were wallowing in it like round-headed hippopotami. It was still daylight, but the light was starting to fade, and it was autumn. Panicking, I dashed downstairs and did the only thing I could think of, which was to line the three lads up and hose them down from head to toe with cold water. Then I marched them to the bathroom and gave them long, hot showers. Rather than being angry, I was impressed by the utter thoroughness with which they had coated themselves.

Fearing the Yoshikawa boys might catch colds from their escapade, I put them in some of Gaku's clothes and escorted them home. Their house was a former electrical appliance store that had recently been converted into a rental unit; it was small, and made of wood and plaster, but it had a yard and a storage shed in the back. Their mother did not seem to be home. Perhaps, I thought, after picking up the children from school she had decided to go shopping.

"Think maybe your mom went to the store?" I asked the two boys. A drain pipe with a dark purple patina ran down beside the front door, and as I watched, Noboru inserted a hand into the opening at the bottom and started groping for something. He seemed to notice me staring at him curiously, for he rolled his little eyes up at me and said, "This is our secret hiding place. You can't look."

"Oh," I said, turning away and suppressing the urge to laugh. The Yoshikawas hid their front door key in the same place as everyone else.

"The key's not there," Noboru announced, staring at the red rust his fingertips had accumulated, "so I don't think she's out on an errand."

"She say she was going somewhere this evening?" I asked.

Noboru silently shook his head, and his brother Kenjiro announced, "I'm cold."

A narrow path ran between the house and a cinderblock wall separating it from the neighbors, so the boys and I slipped around to the backyard. It was extremely modest but well maintained and carefully weeded. The south side of the building had a miniature veranda with a window above it, and on one end of a plastic laundry pole suspended under the eaves, a single pair of tiny tennis shoes had been hung out to dry. The window's rain shutters were closed.

"Mama's bike's still here, so that proves she's not on an errand," Noboru said. "She always uses it, even if she's only going a little ways." Then he put his mouth to a tiny crack between the shutters and yelled, "Mama!"

The autumn sun was quickly sinking, and even I felt cold, so I persuaded the boys to come home with me. When Gaku saw his two pals return he was ecstatic. The three boys immediately glued their faces to the TV set, immersing themselves in the evening cartoon shows while I sat nearby, reading the evening newspaper that had just been delivered.

Fifteen minutes later Kenjiro's mother arrived, looking pale. She appeared to have rushed home, for her shoulders and chest were heaving slightly as if she were out of breath. When she heard what had happened, she was so abject in her apologies that I began to feel sorry for her.

"I'm sorry. I'm terribly sorry," she said. "Something unavoidable came up. I'm sorry. I know these two are real mischief-makers."

"Boys will be boys," I answered, handing her a couple of soaked shirts and short pants, "and they love to play in the mud. It's only normal." I offered to wash the clothes for her, but she refused with a "No, no, you mustn't."

My wife came home right after the Yoshikawas left. She had bought an awful lot of something, for she was carrying three large supermarket shopping bags, and her brow was beaded with sweat. She took her shoes off in the hallway, strode into the house, and immediately asked, "Did you have a visitor?"

I gave her a brief account of what had happened, and as

usual when surprised or curious, her eyes widened and she began to shake her head emphatically from side to side. "What'll those three rascals be up to next!" she said, clearly having enjoyed the story. Then she added in a low voice, as if to herself, "I smell some sort of flower. . . . Smells like fragrant olive."

Sure enough, after that the gang of three kept us constantly entertained. There was no particular ringleader in their high jinks; when they got together, they just naturally seemed to find some interesting "work" to do.

A chicken farm in our area kept its ailing birds in a special coop. I was away when the boys opened the door to it and scattered a dozen of the poor creatures out onto the road, so my wife and Mrs. Yoshikawa had to run around trying desperately to retrieve them. Fortunately, the owner was a kindly old gent who had just been in the process of repairing the coop door, so he said it was an unavoidable accident, and the damage was thus contained.

After the chickens, the lads caused what we called the "sweet potato incident."

One Saturday afternoon in November I brought Gaku back from preschool early. The Yoshikawa boys had also come home early, so he started playing with them as usual. I had some business that day with a publisher some twenty minutes from our house by train, and I thought it was safe to leave for a while.

The day was almost over when my appointment finished and I set off home. My wife had to attend a special training session for teachers at her school, and I had promised to make dinner, so at a market near the railway station I bought some meat, vegetables, and—remembering that we were out of beer—a six-pack. Then I hurried on my way.

When I reached home, I found a mountain of sweet potatoes in front of our gate. They were all caked in dirt, and had clearly just been dug up. While I was still scratching my head, wondering what on earth had happened, sure enough the famous gang of three came charging around from the back yard. And they, too, were caked in dirt, again.

Gaku puffed out his chest and proudly announced, "Look! Look at all the potatoes we got today!"

Kenjiro, with his shrill voice and awkward enunciation, added, "Yeah, Mister Shiina! We all worked together!"

"I see," I said. "And where did get you them?" I suddenly had an inexorable, sinking feeling in my gut. I spun around, and, sure enough, my fear was right on target; part of a field of sweet potatoes in front of our house had been magnificently excavated. "Oh, you kids. . . ," I sputtered. The three mud-caked boys in front of me merely looked prouder and prouder.

That was just the beginning. When I checked, I discovered they had dug up three entire rows of potatoes, which came to a considerable quantity. Noboru ran home to explain to his mother, and she rushed over to see for herself. Clutching her apron with both hands, and looking as though she would burst into tears any minute, she said, "How could they dig up so many?" Then, with the November sun quickly setting and shrouding us in dusk, she looked straight at me with lips drawn tight and tears welling in her eyes. In a hoarse voice she asked, "What should we do?"

"Don't worry," I said. "We'll figure out something." Despite the bravado, I didn't really have much confidence. In our neighborhood, the owner of this particular potato patch was notorious for being an ornery old scrooge, and he had already come over several times to complain about the children trespassing and trampling his field. All I could think of doing was to apologize and give him back his potatoes, or pay for all those the boys had dug up.

Mrs. Yoshikawa and I decided then and there to take the

three criminals to him and apologize. She went home to take off her apron, and returned wearing a pale orange cardigan and carrying jackets for her sons. She took her children by the hand, and as the streetlight bathed her pale orange back, I could see her shoulders were hunched with worry. She seemed very alone to me, but for some utterly inexplicable reason, she also suddenly seemed terribly attractive.

The sweet potato patch owner had just taken an early bath after his day's work, and was vigorously drying his gray-flecked hair with a hand towel. His face had a healthy glow to it. "Well, I don't know about this," he said slowly in a raspy growl that issued from the back of his throat. "You must realize, the only one who understands the true value of the crop is the one who grows it. . . ."

Before he could continue with this Zen-like statement, Kenjiro's mother bowed deeply and said, "I'm terribly sorry, sir. I'm terribly sorry." Then, with her head still lowered, her shoulders began to shake gently, as if she were sobbing.

It irritated me to see this. I felt like yelling out loud that there was absolutely no reason to grovel in such subservient fashion before anyone. No matter what kind of mischief the kids might have been up to, it wasn't as if they had permanently ruined the old man's field. And besides, if it was such a big deal, surely all we needed to do was to buy all the uprooted potatoes at whatever price he demanded.

"Well," the potato patch owner growled, nodding his gray-flecked head. "Well, I reckon if you folks can just understand my situation, maybe I can overlook it this time."

We reached a compromise. The old man agreed to take back half of the potatoes, and we agreed to purchase and keep the other half.

On the way home, whether from empty stomachs, the cold, or a dawning realization that they actually had done something less than laudable, all three boys were unusually quiet. When we arrived in front of Kenjiro and Noboru's house, I made up my mind and said to their mother, "Don't worry, we'll pay for the potatoes. But we can't possibly eat them all, so I'd appreciate it if you'd take half."

"Why, you really shouldn't," she answered, her eyes widening like those of a little girl.

"It's okay. Really."

"But I can't possibly. It's too much. . . ."

"No, I insist. Really. I'd prefer it that way. Besides, it's already late, and the kids are hungry."

I pressed her to accept my proposal. I knew she had probably had to look after her family for years, scrimping and saving, and I wanted to help out in some small way.

When my wife came back later that night I gave her a complete report on the incident.

"So that's what happened," she said, less shocked than I had anticipated. "When I came home and saw that mountain of sweet potatoes under the gate light, I thought something was awfully strange. How much did you have to pay for them?"

"Twenty-eight thousand yen*!"

"Twenty-eight thousand yen? For sweet potatoes?" She rubbed the tip of her nose and suddenly looked terribly interested.

"Yup. And since Kenjiro's family seems to be on a tight budget, I told his mother we'd pay."

"You did?" my wife said. "We're not exactly wealthy either, you know. Hmph! Seems to me like you've got an awfully soft spot for this Mrs. Yoshikawa. Come to think of it, you're always talking about her recently. Come to think of it, you've always liked that type. . . ." The last sentences were delivered

*About $200.

17

with increasing speed.

"Type?" I replied. "What kind of type are you talking about?"

She began rubbing her nose with her index finger again, and wore a mysterious expression somewhere between laughter and pure anger. "Fragrant olive," she said.

The next day, to make sure our son fully understood the seriousness of taking things from the field without permission, my wife initiated a thorough lesson in potato ethics.

"Now, for example, Gaku," she declared in her opening salvo, "if someone takes a lot of potatoes from a potato patch without asking the owner, then that person has to pay for them. Now in your case, because you worked so hard to dig up all those potatoes, we've spent our month's budget on nothing but potatoes, and our house is filled with them, right? So for the time being we're going to have nothing to eat but potatoes. . . ."

And from that day on, everything we ate had sweet potatoes in it. My wife attacked repeatedly with every conceivable dish. We started with sweet potato stew, then had sweet potato tempura, sweet potato miso soup, and mashed sweet potato with sweet chestnuts. For snacks we had steamed sweet potatoes, boiled sweet potato slices fried with honey and sesame, stuffed sweet potato confections, crispy french fried sweet potatoes, and roasted sweet potatoes, ad infinitum.

The potato offensive seemed to have considerable effect, for soon the gang of three began lying low, at least for a while. In the meantime, I occasionally ran into Mrs. Yoshikawa at Gaku's preschool. And as my wife had immediately detected with her keen feminine olfactory sense, it was true that I was becoming more and more attracted to this mysteriously wistful mother of two.

For a diversion one day, when Gaku and the Yoshikawa brothers had finally been liberated from their potato diet, I again tried my hand at an experimental dish and made them a snack of fried thin summer noodles mixed with mayonnaise and soy sauce. And then I once again overheard Noboru suddenly say something that shocked me.

"My daddy died and went to Hell, and I think that guy should, too."

"What?" I exclaimed, letting a fork full of fried noodles drop onto my plate. "What are you talking about?" I was unable to suppress the panic I felt; it sounded as if he were referring to me.

"Oh, I don't mean you, Mister Shiina," he said hastily. "I mean Mister Yoshiro."

"Who's Mister Yoshiro?" I pursued.

"I don't know," Noboru replied with the clearly perturbed look of a wise first grader, "but I don't like him because when he comes over to our place Mama always locks the door from the inside and keeps the key instead of putting it in our usual hiding place. When Mama's bicycle's in front of the house and the door's locked, I know Mister Yoshiro's visiting."

"Oh," I said, slowly scratching the back of my head with my left hand. Somewhere around the area of my heart, I felt a prickly, confused, and sad sensation.

Winter arrived. On the first Saturday in December, on the roof of the preschool building, I finally spoke with Mrs. Yoshikawa again. On Saturday mornings parents were supposed to take the little futon mats their children used for naps up to the school roof to air them. After stripping off the cotton sheet-covers, they would hang the mats on the roof railing; then they would take the covers home to wash and bring them back the following Monday. The housewives who also took the children to and from school normally did this sort of chore. Initially I felt a bit embarrassed about it.

Kenjiro's mother hung her futon out on the railing, beat it lightly, and pulled the corners taut. Then, on her way back to the roof door, she came over to me. "Er. . . ," she said, bowing slightly, "I . . . I heard you made the boys a special treat of noodles the other day. I just wanted to thank you again for always being so kind."

"No, no, think nothing of it," I said, feeling flustered for some reason.

"Special noodles sounds great," she said, looking much more cheerful than usual. "By the way, this is rather sudden, but I just wanted to tell you I'll be moving soon. . . ."

"Oh," I said.

Perhaps because the breeze was blowing away from me that morning, I couldn't detect a trace of her usual fragrant olive perfume.

"Where are you moving to?" I asked.

"Well, we, ah, it's not. . . ." She didn't complete her sentence. "I just wanted to tell you," she continued, "how happy I was that Kenjiro and Noboru had a friend so close by. They got into an awful lot of mischief, but they sure seemed to have a lot of fun in the process."

I wasn't sure why, but I laughed. And in the light of that early winter morning, Kenjiro's mother gave a little laugh, too. In fact, I realized it was the first time I had ever seen her really look happy.

The day Kenjiro Yoshikawa came to say goodbye, Gaku announced that he was going to give him his stuffed brontosaurus. It was a green dinosaur with a ferocious expression but surprisingly gentle eyes.

Standing in front of the entrance to our house with his rucksack on, looking very serious, Kenjiro announced with his usual shrill voice and funny enunciation, "I'm gonna go to a place called I-ru-ma district." His brother Noboru, standing at attention beside him and speaking stiffly as if he were reading from a Japanese-language textbook, added, "Please come and visit us

20

sometime, Gaku!" I wondered if his mother had coached him only a few minutes earlier on exactly what to say.

"If the brontosaurus gets dirty," Gaku said, "you can wash him in the bath, you know."

"I know that," Kenjiro replied, flushing.

Then Kenjiro and his brother, both acting as if they had just been rehearsed by their mother, bowed their shaved heads simultaneously and said, "Goodbye, Mister Shiina. Goodbye, Gaku."

"Goodbye," Gaku answered, a little formally.

Kenjiro's mother never came by our house. She apparently left straight for the "I-ru-ma" district.

Swallowtails

Whic we were taking a bath one day, Gaku suddenly asked, "Pa, am I bald?"

He looked far too worried for me to laugh. "No, Gaku," I said, "you're definitely not bald."

"Really? But Yuji and the others keep calling me "Baldy.' "

"Hmm. Well, your head's shaved, Gaku, but you're not bald. Baldies don't have any hair on their head."

"Oh," he said, as though he had resolved something within himself. "That's good."

I've shaved Gaku's head almost since his birth. At first I used to take him to the barbershop when his hair grew out, but I soon tired of that. It seemed ridiculous to pay 1,600 yen* to shave such a tiny head, so I went out and bought some electric hair clippers,

*About $12.00.

and after stripping him I gave his noggin a quick once-over in the bathroom. In the beginning it was hard to get the knack of using just the right pressure or speed, and I often made him squeal. But after three years of practice, I finally got to the point where I could buzz his head in no time flat, and even feel ready to take on two or three more mop-tops.

Something bothered me about his question, so I asked him, "What's so 'good' about not being bald?"

"Well, you know Yuji, he keeps calling me 'Baldy,' 'Baldy.' So today I punched him one."

He was standing in the wash area outside the tub, looking at me with a terribly serious expression as he said this. Then he started vigorously scrubbing the nape of his neck with his soaped-up washcloth. I already knew that he was the only one in his class with a shaved head.

"So you hit him, eh?" I asked.

"Yeah."

"And then what happened?"

"He started bawling."

"No kidding."

"Yeah."

"Yuji's a classmate of yours?"

"No."

"What class is he in?"

"He's a third grader. His name's Yuji Yoshino, and he's in class 3-A."

"I see."

For a while I stared in silence at my son's round head; it would be another two weeks before he needed his next haircut. Then I suddenly remembered the first semester report card the rascal had brought home in first grade. His terrible grades had not surprised me, but the comments under the heading "Observations on Social Development" had. "Young Gaku appears to have a rather violent streak in him," his teacher had written. "When I asked his classmates how many had been hit by him, nearly two-thirds raised their hands."

When my wife had seen the report card, she had turned noticeably pale and had said not a word. Only later that spring night—spring only in name, for the night air was still nippy—had she finally whispered to me, "Do you think we're raising him wrong?"

"No, I don't think that's the problem," I answered, trying to view the situation in the best possible light. "Don't worry, he'll be fine." I knew the worried words "raising him wrong" stemmed from her insecurity about our basic qualifications as parents.

A year before Gaku started elementary school, my wife and I had talked it over and decided not to put him in any of the special preparatory courses that were fashionable for preschoolers. We live in a typical Tokyo suburban bedroom community, filled with stuck-up families obsessed with rearing their children in the "proper" way. Our community is, in short, exactly the sort of environment the so-called education mamas of Japan love to inhabit, the sort of place where hordes of them shamelessly besiege kindergarten teachers with disgusting questions, such as: "How much should we make our child master before he enters school?" "What should we have him study?" "What should his comprehension level be?" "People say it's best to learn English conversation at an early age, so don't you think we should start him off soon? What's your advice, Teacher?"

For better or for worse, Gaku had gone to a freewheeling public preschool where the teachers were so obsessed with the struggle to raise their salaries they had little time to worry about the pupils. He was thus spared teachers with a weird zeal for silly "pretend-study" sessions, and instead had a great time. He ran around with his pals all day long, and then came home to roughhouse with his boring dad and pretend he was a professional wrestler or boxer.

Soon after Gaku entered elementary school, I realized that nowadays most parents drill their children in a variety of lessons at home before they start school. None of his first grade classmates had any problem reading their *hiragana* phonetic characters, and many were even able to write them with ease. Sure enough (or true to form), out of a class of thirty-four, my son was the only one unable to read or write at all.

A couple of months later, while we were taking a bath, I had asked him if he enjoyed his new school. Yeah, he had said, his expression lighting up, it was fun. But preschool was more fun because he hadn't had to study. Then, as I watched, he seemed to re-think his priorities, for he responded brightly that elementary school was actually more fun because he got to play real soccer.

The second semester began before my wife and I could figure out what to do about the havoc noted on Gaku's first semester report card. To Gaku, the biggest thrill of school was the chance to play with his pals, and then after school to run around at full tilt with a dozen of them until dark. But in the second semester this became more and more difficult, for several of his friends started after-school piano lessons or English conversation classes. And, unfortunately, the number of places where children could run around freely began to decrease dramatically.

After 3:40 on weekday afternoons, it was ruled that no one was allowed to use the school yard; the teachers closed the gates and told the children to go home. On Sundays, the school began loaning out its grounds to baseball and soccer teams from the city, but, afraid of liability if any injuries should occur, it prohibited its own students from using them.

Around the same time, many of the ordinary vacant lots around the city also succumbed to a fad. A variant of croquet, called "gateball," had become all the rage among senior citizens, and under city policy more and more vacant lots were transformed into gateball courts for them. Barbed wire was strung around these courts, and even if children tried to use them after the seniors were finished, they were shooed away, apparently from a fear that they would mess up the surface of the courts.

As he was lying on his bed one day, looking out of sorts, Gaku called to me: "Pa," he said. (Most Japanese children use more formal words for "father" and "mother," but ever since he was a baby, Gaku had just said the equivalent of "pa" and "ma," dropping the honorific "san." When I asked him why, he always replied in utter seriousness that we weren't famous enough for the "san.")

"Pa," he again said with a pout. "You know what? When I went to the park today, they'd already turned the place into gateball courts. Now the only place we can play baseball is in Central Park, but when we go there the grown-ups get angry and say we can't play."

"That park's really being ruined, isn't it?" was my comment.

"Central Park" had once been an enormous expanse of huge ginkgo trees and mulberry orchards, an experimental site for growing mountain mulberry, but the city had plowed most of the site under to create a broad grassy field. And that was fine with me. When Gaku was still in preschool, I used to go there every Sunday with him. The field was so big it had four sandlot baseball diamonds—usually filled from early morning with local teams battling one another—and in the few open spaces on the periphery children would play their own games of baseball and soccer. It was an ideal place for people in the neighborhood to walk their dogs, and many grown-ups with time on their hands also gathered there simply to stroll about or watch the games.

Just before summer vacation, when the children were really

looking forward to some serious playing, the city suddenly closed off the space, and large numbers of dump trucks and bulldozers materialized. As it turned out, they were going to construct an "official" public park.

Construction continued for a year and a half. They dug up the vast grassy field, laid concrete around it, and transformed the central area into a deluxe stadium complete with tiered stands for spectators. Then they turned the few open areas around the stadium into sites for track and field, tennis and gateball courts, and flowerbeds bordered with bricks to keep people off. It was said that 4 billion yen had already been spent to develop this "Grand Public Park," and that another 6 billion would be needed to finish it.

When part of the new park was opened to the public, Gaku and I went to take a look. There was a huge sign at the entrance, looking for all the world like an edict posted for the townspeople by a magistrate in feudal days. On a big, one-meter-square board, fat red and black characters announced: "Dogs and Cats Prohibited."

"What's it say?" Gaku asked.

"Well, it says dogs and cats can't come in here."

"Hmm," the tyke said. Then he thought it over very seriously, and quickly added, "But that's weird."

"Why?"

"How can dogs and cats read?"

A-hah, I thought, he's right. People usually walked their dogs on a leash, so the sign clearly could be directed at them, but cats ran about on their own, wherever and whenever they pleased.

"You're right," I said, laughing. "How in the world could a cat read this sign?"

Gaku had finally advanced to the point where he no longer scrawled his hiragana characters back to front or upside down, and he could actually write them correctly. "Yeah," he said, grinning happily because he felt a tad smarter than a cat. "What a stupid sign!"

The city authorities love to prohibit things arbitrarily, but the logic for banning cats and dogs from the park was beyond me. There was something farcical about their actions in general, something that rubbed me the wrong way.

They had transformed our former grassy expanse into a multipurpose athletic facility. On the other side of a playing field, they had created a three-hundred-meter-long oval track, and when Gaku and I rounded it, we came upon yet another odd sight—a shot put circle, such as school sports fields often had in the old days.

"Look at this, Gaku," I said. "This is where they practice shot put."

He didn't seem very interested. A helicopter was flying above the other side of the field, beyond the grove of ginkgo trees, over an area that would soon be turned into a gymnasium. As we strolled by the shot put circle, I couldn't help thinking that, to my disgust, although the park was supposed to be for the "public," the planners seemed determined to alienate the real public. The shot put circle was an excellent case in point. Of all the local people, how many actually practiced shot put? As far as I was concerned, instead of creating a fancy space for a few athletic club members who practiced once or twice a year, they should have made a space for kids and animals to run around and play in every day. I thought about it as Gaku and I strolled around, and the more I thought about it, the more depressed I felt about the place I was living in.

Gaku entered second grade after spring vacation in April, which is when the new school year starts in Japan. It occurred to me belatedly that although I had asked him as a first grader why he hit his classmates, he had never given me a real answer. He had scraped by a whole year as the only illiterate ignoramus in a class of thirty-four. Perhaps, I thought, the young man simply had too many other things to worry about.

In second grade, Gaku's biggest thrill in school continued to be the chance to romp with his pals. He would get together with a group of them every day, find a place to play, and engage in all kinds of antics. He often talked about his games when we were taking a bath together, and soon he began mentioning a classmate called Takayama with ever-greater frequency. I had never heard of this friend before, and when I asked, he replied that Takayama was a new student who had just joined his class. Then, in the midst of relating how he had hit Yuji, the third grader, a year before, he started talking about Takayama again. Apparently he had been going over to Takayama's house to play.

"Takayama really knows lots about fishing," he said proudly, almost as if he were boasting about himself. "He's got a brother in fifth grade, and they go fishing with their dad a lot. They've got tons of huge fishing poles at their place."

Takayama was apparently quite a generous lad, for Gaku started coming home with all sorts of things after visiting him, including fancy fishing plugs, fishing line, odd-shaped fishing floats, and even plastic model toys.

While on a walk through the woods by Central Park one day, I asked Gaku, "Seems like Takayama gives you an awful lot of nice things. You ever give him anything?"

"Yeah," he said. "Once I gave him my Grandizer super-alloy robot kit. But I think he likes to give me stuff more."

We were looking for a special citron tree that day. The city had partitioned off part of Central Park with an inelegant steel fence during the construction, and the woods had been reduced to nearly half their previous size, but we nonetheless found the tree we were looking for. It was a little dusty, but it was standing in its usual spot, all by itself.

"Look!" Gaku yelled, dashing around the tree, "There's lots of "em."

At first I couldn't see what he was referring to. But then, on the dark green underside of one of the tree's leaves, just where the stem forked, I saw dozens of tiny hairy caterpillars squirming about.

We put twenty or so caterpillars into a paper bag we had brought along with us and tossed in a bunch of leaves from the tree for them to feed on. It was sort of a fad among children of Gaku's age to catch these larvae, and then raise them until they eventually were transformed into butterflies.

"Your friend Takayama raise caterpillars, too?" I asked.

"Naw. He's raising tropical fish with his brother. They've got a bunch of 'em in a huge tank. He said his dad brings 'em back from overseas."

On the way back, Gaku held the paper bag up to his ear and exclaimed, "I can hear 'em! I can hear 'em eating the leaves!"

I met Gaku's friend for the first time a week later, when he came over to play on a Saturday. He had what appeared to be a plastic model pistol in his right hand, and a casting rod with a reel in his left. He was a size smaller than Gaku, and wore shorts with a cute apple design in appliqué-which looked childish even on a second grader. And in complete contrast to Gaku, with his close-shaven head, he wore his hair in a girlish pageboy style. They made quite a pair.

"So," I said, poking my head out of the living room. "You must be the Takayama lad. Come on in."

"Thank you. Begging your pardon, sir," he said in a squeaky, tinny voice. Then he removed his shoes in accordance with Japanese custom and stepped up from the hallway into the room.

"You put that pistol together yourself?" I asked.

"Yes, sir," he replied.

I toyed with the idea of asking him to let me have a look at it so I could check it out, but I decided not to. He spoke in such an adult, formal fashion for a second grader that joshing him didn't seem appropriate. If he wasn't going to use language like "yeah," "um," and "you know," it would just be too awkward.

"It's awfully kind of you to give Gaku so many nice things," I said, "so please allow me to fry some delicious noodles for you later in return." The boy's overly proper speech had thrown me off balance. I was having trouble talking normally.

"Thank you, sir," he answered in his shrill voice. Then he followed Gaku upstairs.

Something bothered me about all this. I had difficulty believing that modern second graders normally said, "Begging your pardon, sir," and I sincerely questioned whether my son—the swaggering Gaku—would conduct himself as politely when visiting someone else's house. I resolved to ask him directly after the Takayama lad had left, but I was distracted by other matters that day and forgot all about it.

A month into Gaku's first semester as a second grader, an "incident" occurred. I was at home when I suddenly got a call from his school.

"I'm sorry to bother you," said his teacher, Mr. Yamagishi, "but we need you or your wife to come to the school right away." His voice was oddly muffled, as if he were covering the mouthpiece of the receiver with his hand.

My wife had already come home after working the early shift that day. When I told her about the call, she looked extremely worried. "What on earth can it be?" she said.

"I'm sure Gaku hasn't been hurt," I replied, "or Mr. Yamagishi would have made it sound much more urgent."

My wife left for school and returned with our son an hour later. Her face was flushed around the bridge of her nose, and she was clearly exhausted. As soon as Gaku ran upstairs to his

31

bedroom and was out of earshot, she turned to me, speaking quickly in a low voice: "You know what? They say Gaku stole money from his friend."

"What?" I exclaimed. The teacher's call had worried me, but I had assumed that it was just about another fight with a friend, or that he and his pals had been caught in some new mischief. Her words stunned me.

"Mrs. Takayama apparently went to the school in a huff," she continued. "She said her elder son's allowance keeps disappearing, so last night she asked her youngest about it, and he said Gaku's been stealing it."

"You mean she really thinks Gaku went to their house to steal?" I was shocked, but part of me felt like laughing at the very absurdity of the idea.

"That's right. She said it couldn't possibly be her own son. She made a real scene!"

"I can't believe it."

"It was such a shock I could hardly believe my own ears, either. We haven't even heard Gaku's side of the story yet."

"What did Gaku's teacher say?"

"That we should look into the matter."

I was painfully aware of my mood suddenly turning indescribably dark. I knew what was bothering me more than anything else, so I asked, "How can Mrs. Takayama be so damned sure Gaku took the money?"

"Well, when I pressed her, she said that's what her son had told her."

A sudden image of the Takayama lad with his pageboy haircut flashed into my mind. As my wife recounted it, Mrs. Takayama believed Gaku had stolen a five-hundred-yen note-a crisp new bill-that her elder boy had been planning to put in his savings account. But that was not all. Some fishing lures and floats he treasured had also been regularly disappearing of late,

32

and Gaku had apparently taken them, too, she said. Her son's belongings were one thing, she had proclaimed in front of the teacher and my wife, her shrill voice rising in anger, but the money was another. It was extremely serious when a boy of Gaku's age began "stealing money"!

People often say they experience chest pains when greatly upset or angered, and I've decided they're right. As I listened to my wife's account, I could feel my heart slowly, painfully contracting.

That night, while taking a bath with Gaku, I asked him point-blank: "Say, Gaku, did you ever take any fishing lures or money from the Takayama place without asking?"

I deliberately made my voice as normal as possible, and—though it was a bit awkward—even tried to sound as if I were joking.

Gaku was busy making a mass of bubbles with his washcloth. "Yeah," he said, all too easily.

"Without asking?" I demanded immediately. I had a sinking feeling in the pit of my stomach.

"It wasn't me," he said. "Takayama got the stuff himself. That's what he said. And then he gave it to me."

"The money, too?"

"Sure. He gave me five hundred and thirty yen the other day."

"What'd you do with it?"

"Me and Kei and Takayama and Imai's older brother, we all went over to the Medakaya store and played with the 'clackety machine.'"

The "clackety machine" he referred to was a little vending machine. When two or three ten-yen coins were inserted and a handle turned, it disgorged tiny prizes in clear plastic containers.

"You used all five hundred and thirty yen?"

"Sure. We each got to play about three times. And then

Imai's brother—you know what!—he got the same thing three times, so he got angry and shook the machine, so then the man in the store got mad at us. I'm good at it, though. I got a different prize each time."

Gaku looked supremely unconcerned as he spoke.

"Gaku, the money and the fishing things didn't belong to your friend. They belonged to his elder brother. From now on, even if he tells you he's giving you something, I want you to say no. Understand?" For the first time I used a fairly sharp tone.

"How come?"

"Because I say so. And you're never to let a friend give you money."

"Okay," he replied simply.

"You ever have a fight with Takayama?"

"Nope. Never."

"You ever hit him?"

"No. He's my friend. Why should I hit him?"

"You're a pretty good fighter, aren't you, Gaku?"

"Yeah. Not bad, I guess."

"The strongest in the class?"

"Yeah."

"In your whole grade?"

"I suppose so. It's a toss-up between me or Kyoichi in 2-B. Kyoichi's pretty good, too."

As Gaku replied to my questions in his typically direct manner, I couldn't help chuckling to myself. After all, I had spent most of my time with him, not making him study but playing at boxing, karate, and professional wrestling. No wonder the subject in which the rascal had made the greatest progress was fighting.

Three days later, at my wife's suggestion, I went to Gaku's school to speak with his teacher. I wanted to learn a little more about what had actually happened, and to apologize in my own way for the problems I was sure he was causing, even in normal circumstances.

Mr. Yamagishi was in his fifties, and looked and sounded like a true veteran. "Well, he's still a young lad," he said calmly, "and nearly all of us are tested like this once or twice in our lives."

At first I couldn't figure out what type of test he was talking about, but as he continued I realized everything he said was based on the assumption that his pupil—my son, Gaku—was indeed the criminal in the incident. I was outraged, and felt at a loss for words. It was as if I were listening to a Sunday school teacher delivering a sermon on morality to a repentant pupil. I couldn't believe it.

As far as I was concerned, Mrs. Takayama's story was crazy. For the life of me, I simply could not imagine my easygoing son sneaking into the elder Takayama boy's room like a professional thief and stealing a crisp new five-hundred-yen note from his desk drawer. After all, I gave this same son of mine a monthly allowance of one hundred and fifty yen in coins, and he always left them scattered over his desk because he never spent them all! Why in the world would he steal? I trembled with rage at the very thought of Mrs. Takayama's accusation.

After my discussion with Gaku in the bath three days earlier, I thought I finally understood what had really happened, but because I was the "parent" in this case, I didn't feel it would be proper for me to tell Mr. Yamagishi my true suspicions. In fact, I was convinced that the Takayama boy—the wimpy-looking new student with a pageboy haircut—had actually been trying to butter up the toughest fighter in his class by bringing him some tribute.

"Well," Mr. Yamagishi continued, "much to my relief, this time the other lad's parents have decided that if you and your wife do your best to ensure that this type of incident is not repeated, it's in the best interest of both children not to pursue the matter further."

He seemed to be trying to impress me, for his eyes flashed behind his glasses, and he finally lit the long cigarette he had been twirling between his fingers.

That evening, when my wife came back from work, I burst into the room where she was changing and blurted out, "It's terrible. They're already treating Gaku like a criminal." The whole matter was depressing me no end.

As usual, Gaku and I took a bath before dinner and had a man-to-man chat.

"You know what?" he said, soaking up to his shoulders in the bath and slowly shaking his shaved head from left to right. "When I checked my insect cage today, three of the caterpillars looked like maybe they were dead. But eighteen of them have made cocoons."

"No kidding," I said. "That happened awful fast, didn't it."

"Yeah. It's because I give 'em lots of food every day. I watched 'em, and sure enough, the ones that ate the most turned into cocoons first. Komatsu and Ma-chan say their caterpillars have turned into cocoons, too, but I bet mine'll be the first to become butterflies."

"No kidding."

"Yeah," Gaku said, crinkling the skin between his eyebrows in a frown, and answering me with a terribly adult expression, "And you know what? Takayama told me today he'd give me some caterpillars that turn into gossamer-wing butterflies, but I said I didn't want them. They're not cool."

"Oh. Gossamer wings aren't cool, are they?"

"No. They're little, and not cool."

I looked at Gaku's serious expression, and couldn't help smiling. "No kidding," I said.

A week later, the swallowtail butterflies in Gaku's insect

cage began to emerge from their cocoons all at once.

"Pa! They made it!" Gaku yelled exuberantly as he bounded down the stairs, waving his right hand triumphantly. "There's exactly thirteen right now. At this rate they'll all come out of their cocoons and turn into butterflies!"

I went up to my son's room on the second floor. Overnight, the eighteen pupae in the tiny insect cage atop his desk had all begun to transform into swallowtail butterflies, which had practically no room to move and stretch their new wings. A mass of black and yellow wings was flapping furiously. As I watched, it seemed almost as though the little cage was going to start rocking back and forth, and then slowly lift off into the air.

"Amazing, huh?" Gaku said. "It's like all of 'em are turning into swallowtails at once." He held the cage in both hands, and, with a happily bemused look, stood still for a moment, seemingly at a loss what to do.

Around noon the next day, Gaku stood on the second-floor veranda and tried to free the new swallowtails. At first some merely flapped their wings futilely and refused to fly, even though the door to the tiny cage was open. But then two or three, as if it were the most natural thing in all the world, found their own way to the little square door of the cage and poised on the edge. Then they sprang forth into the air and flew off.

With a "Hooray!" Gaku thrust the cage out over the veranda railing and yelled, "Here you go! Fly! Fly away!"

As I watched, standing next to my shaven-headed boy, the rest of the swallowtails beat their still-shaky wings and fluttered gently up into the hot, humid air of a sunny summer afternoon.

THREE

A Horn From India

Ibought the horn at a bicycle shop in Calcutta. It was made of sturdy tin, curled around like a ram's horn at one end with a big rubber bulb at the other; giving the bulb a good hard squeeze drove air through the horn and created a loud, goofy noise like a bellowing oaf.

The first time I visited Calcutta, the sound of these horns nearly overwhelmed me. "Bicycle rickshaws," human-powered like those of old Japan, vastly outnumber automobiles, and they all have these horns attached. As the rickshaws race through the jam-packed streets of the city, the horns constantly blare BLAT-BLET, BLAT-BLET.

The moment I saw one of these horns I remembered a man I knew once, long ago, when I was still in elementary school. He was a scrap collector, who had a workhorse type of bicycle with a big luggage rack. He used to pull a cart with sides of plywood board and ride around town ever so slowly, at about half the speed at which a man would normally walk. Everyone in my town knew him as Sanzo of Kameya. Since I was a child then and never learned with what characters he wrote his name, I do not know what the "Kameya" meant. It could have referred either to a place called "Kameya," or to a shop. In those days in our half-fishing, half-farming village, it was common to call people by the name of the store or business they were connected with, rather than by their real names. At any rate, to us he was just "Sanzo of Kameya."

Why did I suddenly recall this man in far-off Calcutta? Because I remembered as clear as day that on the handlebars of the sturdy bicycle which he used to pull his cart around town, he had a big horn that he honked incessantly. And it was almost exactly like those in India.

In my childhood memories of him, Sanzo of Kameya seems more like an old man than a big grown-up, but judging from the many stories that surround him I suspect that he was only in his late forties or early fifties. He was heavy-set, and always wore tall rubber boots and a torn workman's dark-colored jacket. He probably looked especially old to me at the time because he sported a disheveled, untamed beard that sprouted all over his swarthy face. He may also have been a little crazy. He rarely spoke while collecting scrap, and when looking for an odd job he always mumbled in an irritatingly slow, low voice, "Sorry to bother you. Want me to chop some wood for you?"

The town children called him either "Kame" or "Sanzo." The women called him by the more friendly "Kame-san," and some asked him to chop wood for them and paid him for his time. He may have been unwashed and lacking in intelligence, but he had a gentle personality that reminded me of a water buffalo standing submissively in the middle of a rice paddy; he never became mean or violent, even when upset. Since he performed a variety of hard physical chores for a pittance, he was especially prized in households that were short of grown men. Many depended on him, and put out scrap for him to collect several times a month. It was an example, one might say, of the almost-good-old-days of Japan, when people were bound together in a true community.

In the heat, din, and utterly raw energy of the streets of Calcutta, the faces of the rickshaw drivers who delighted in the loud, excessive use of their horns began to overlap in my mind with the hairy, swarthy face of Sanzo of Kameya.

During the three or so days I spent walking around Calcutta, I always had a guide named Janakiram, from the government tourist agency. Short and plump for an Indian, he had gentle eyes and spoke fluent Japanese, and after three days together he reminded me less and less of a government bureaucrat, and more and more of an extremely friendly and garrulous owner of a souvenir shop.

I mentioned that I wanted one of the rickshaw horns.

"Ah, no problem, Mr. Shiina," Janakiram said with a smile. "Sometimes blokes like you want to buy them to take home as a souvenir, but they come in all prices. Let me show you. . . ."

He slipped into a bazaar that happened to be right in front of us, in a dark, covered arcade on the edge of town, and he led me to a souvenir shop deep in a back street where I suspect few tourists ever ventured. On a wall of the shop, along with several old Hindu idols, was an orange-colored horn of the type I wanted.

"How much is it?" Janakiram asked the shopkeeper.

The shopkeeper, a young man with a funny-looking goatee, suddenly turned his head and answered in a oddly low voice, "One hundred and twenty rupees." Since one rupee was around twenty-five Japanese yen, that meant it came to about three thousand yen.*

*About $25.00.

Janakiram whispered to me, keeping his eye on the shop-keeper's face, "Well?" he said. "See how expensive it is? This fellow's asking for the moon."

We immediately left the shop. From a Japanese perspective, three thousand yen for a such a fine horn certainly didn't seem much. Since I wanted the thing so badly, it even seemed like a bargain. But I knew the cost of living in Calcutta was completely different than in Japan. Before going to the bazaar that day, in fact, Janakiram and I had looked around the movie theaters in town, where tickets sold for two rupees, or fifty yen. From this, even I could tell that the shopkeeper had jacked the price of his horn way up in hopes of making a killing off a tourist.

Janakiram and I walked out of the store into the dusty, wind-blown streets of Calcutta, but I kept thinking about the shopkeeper, his pointed goatee, and the shady, almost criminal look in his eyes. Something about his expression again made me think of Sanzo of Kameya.

Kame-san was usually irritatingly slow, but when he pedaled past our house he always squeezed the rubber bulb of his horn and honked energetically. From the BLET-BLET sound, I could tell he was passing even if I were playing inside.

Whenever the children in my town were disobedient or cried too much, their mothers always admonished them with a "If you don't stop that, Kame-san'll come." To most little children, he was such a mysterious, scary person that the very words were enough to make them cower in fear and whimper, "No! No! I'm scared of him!" and do whatever they were asked. For the mothers in our town at least, Sanzo of Kameya was a very convenient fellow to have around.

When Kame-san came by to solicit wood-chopping chores or for his main job of collecting scrap, the children often ran in terror inside the house to stare at him from behind the safety of a door. But when the same children reached fourth or fifth grade,

Kame-san no longer seemed so frightening, or at least they stopped running away. Instead they started saying, "Who's afraid of Kame-san?" This, in fact, became one of the yardsticks used to measure how sophisticated we were.

One day at the beginning of summer, when I was in the fifth grade and starting to figure out how the real world worked, Kame-san came to our house and scared the wits out of me. My mother probably had a pile of old newspapers or rags that she wanted to get rid of, for when he passed by honking BLET-BLET as usual, she called out for him to stop. The noon air was already hot and sticky, but he had his tight-sleeved workman's jacket on. He normally never took it off until midsummer, and, even more mysterious to a child like me, on a scorching day he could be chopping wood with his jacket on and not sweat a drop.

The gate in front of our house was fashioned from iron pipes, and when Kame-san opened it, he announced in a mournfully low voice, "Scuse me," and came in. I could see him clearly, because I was standing right in front of him.

His hair was unkempt, his beard was as wild as that of Shoki, the fierce plague-fighting Chinese deity, and his eyes were a blazing, bright red. Although the summer sun itself was blinding, his eyes seemed to flash angrily, and for a second he looked more like a mysterious monster than a human being. The sensation was so powerful that I found myself blurting out in a funny voice, "Aiee!" I began trembling, and crouched down in fear in front of our door.

The sun seemed especially glaring after Janakiram and I emerged from that shadowy bazaar in Calcutta. The summer light in India, I found, had an openly hostile quality to it, and it seared the stones and dirt of the bone-dry streets.

Janakiram pulled a neatly folded square handkerchief out of

his pants' pocket, carefully patted the back of his neck, and glanced up at the sky as if to check the sun's position. "I know another place so cheap you won't believe it," he said as we walked.

"Really?" I said. "Where is it?"

"On the west side of town," he answered. "It's really not far, but if you'd like to go, let's take rickshaws."

The back alleys of Calcutta teem with people, cows, dogs, carts, bicycles, and rickshaws, all in motion, and our rickshaws cut through the crowds at such a reckless speed that it made me cringe. My driver appeared to be a lad of no more than twelve or thirteen. Clad in a sleeveless undershirt, with a dhoti wrapped around his waist like a pair of shorts, he pedaled furiously, rotating a huge drive chain. And whenever another rickshaw came from the left or right through the crowd he blasted them with a mighty BLAM-BLEM of his horn.

After traveling for fifteen minutes or so through the back streets, we suddenly came upon what appeared to be a traffic circle in the road. Janakiram, who had been traveling ahead of me in his own rickshaw, signaled me to dismount.

I got out of my rickshaw and looked around. The traffic circle was surrounded by what looked like bicycle and rickshaw repair shops, with an occasional hardware shop here and there. Janakiram entered one of the shops and began talking in Hindi. I heard his unique, breathy hyeh-hyeh laugh, and soon afterwards he beckoned me to enter, too. There were dozens of tin horns hanging from the roof of the store, all the same shape but each painted a slightly different color.

"Take your pick," he said, fingering the end of his beard. "You can have any one of them for thirty rupees."

Thirty rupees was equivalent to seven hundred and fifty Japanese yen—indeed, one-fourth of the price of the store in the shadowy bazaar earlier—but I nearly burst out laughing, for

Janakiram looked so terribly proud of himself.

I purchased a green-colored horn after making sure that it had a good sound. When its rubber diaphragm was squeezed, it bleated mournfully with a tone reminiscent of tearing wax paper: BURBLEP-BURBLEP.

At the end of the same summer when I had seen Kame-san's flashing red eyes, I heard that he had attacked the Chidori lady. This astonishing news spread through my elementary school (I was in fifth grade) like wildfire, more or less in the form of, "Kame hit the Chidori lady and hurt her, and then he ran to the sea where he was caught by the police."

Chidori, or Plover, was the name of a seaside lodge in our town, and the lady who ran it was the mistress of a man who had a local starch factory. Our town was a popular spot for gathering shellfish along the beach, and people flocked to it during the holiday season, so we had a whole row of seaside lodges whose foundation pillars jutted out into the water. The Chidori was said to be one of the most popular of all.

The Chidori was a little unusual in that it had a pub-like space in the corner of its lounge area, where saké was served along with oden stew and grilled clams. Because of the alcohol, the Chidori was filled with good-ol'-boys from town who came to drink, even on cloudy weekdays when there were hardly any beachcombers around.

I didn't realize it until many years later, but despite the fact that the mistress of the Chidori was past her prime, she was apparently regarded in our town as an unusually attractive woman. I saw her many times, of course, but to my immature eyes her heavily made-up face appeared unnaturally white, and I frankly thought she looked a little weird. But I do remember a brother six years older saying later that she was really too beautiful for our town, so her reputation must have been well deserved.

One of my most interesting memories of her lodge and the others is that they charged money to watch professional wrestling matches on television. This was around the time that the immensely popular wrestler Riki Dozan created the first "Golden Age" of professional wrestling in Japan, and even the Japan Broadcasting Corporation—the public channel—relayed the matches; when really important matches were held, both it and the commercial stations would broadcast them during prime time for three days running.

Most people did not have televisions in those days, so they crowded around sets on street corners or in electrical appliance stores. The seaside lodges were quick to take advantage of this fascination with the new medium, but the Chidori was the first actually to get a large set and charge admission to see the wrestling matches. Both children and adults paid ten yen, or the equivalent of about one hundred yen today, and crowds of up to three hundred people immediately gathered to watch. Considering that the TV just sat there and automatically received the images, collecting money from three hundred people for an hour's viewing was a brilliant idea. And the person who thought this up was doubtless the very capable, beautiful mistress of the Chidori lodge.

In a town where nothing much ever happened, the bizarre news that the beautiful mistress of the Chidori had been attacked by Kame-san created an enormous uproar. My first thought when I heard it was of his blood-red eyes that I had seen earlier. I shuddered when I thought of what he might have done with those eyes to the mistress of the Chidori.

For some reason, neither the radio nor the local newspaper even mentioned the incident, and I had to get all my information about it from my classmates by word-of-mouth the next day. And the reports were confusing. Kame-san, they said, had assaulted the mistress of the Chidori and then fled into the ocean, taking advantage of the low tide to go as far out as possible. But then the tide had turned and started coming in, and by the time it reached his neck, he had been caught by the police in a boat. With his wild hair soaked in seawater, he had merely stood and roared at them like a cornered tiger or lion. Neither my classmates nor I had any idea who had actually seen these goings-on, or how, but the sensational reports kept pouring in.

Shortly afterwards, Kame-san disappeared altogether. And despite the scandal, the mistress of the Chidori continued living in her lodge and powdering her face white as usual. I knew Kame-san was supposed to have done something outrageous to her, yet clearly she hadn't been horribly injured or disfigured. With the limited information available around school, my classmates and I were merely left to wonder why Kame-san was no longer around.

Kame-san returned to our town around five years later. I was in high school by that time, so my memory of him from then is clearer than when I was in elementary school. He was completely changed, and no longer the Kame-san we had once known.

To start with, he had lost an enormous amount of weight. And he had lopped off his wild hair, which gave him a forlorn, bald look. And no matter how you looked at his eyes, they weren't red. They were cloudy and mud-yellow, as if he were somehow ill.

One thing hadn't changed. He still pulled a cart with his work-horse bicycle, and he still rode slowly around, constantly honking BLET-BLET. After a five-year absence it was surprising that he still had the bicycle, but I suppose the police had impounded it and kept it all that time.

I still didn't know whether Sanzo of Kameya had actually attacked the mistress of the Chidori or not. If he had, one could assume that he had been in jail for five years, but since the "victim" in this case appeared to be doing absolutely fine, a five-year jail sentence somehow seemed excessive. And no matter how one looked at it, Kame-san's mental condition was not exactly normal, so one had to question the appropriateness of sentencing him in the same way as normal people.

The new Kame-san put his skills to work and started his scrap business again, but now that he was known for his violence, fewer homes asked for his services the way they had before. Times had also changed, and dealing in scrap wasn't as viable a business as it had once been. Soon Kame-san gave up collecting scrap with his bicycle and cart.

Around the same time, the Chidori lodge was torn down. It wasn't the only one. The authorities had been promoting a shore reclamation project for a long time, and they had finally concluded negotiations with the fishermen for their loss of income. The fishermen in the town decided to give up their livelihood and accept the compensation offered them, and when they did that, all the seaside lodges were soon torn down, too. Since the landfill operation hadn't started, people would still have come to hunt for shellfish during the holiday season even though the fishermen had left, but the owners of the lodges had all apparently decided to get out of the business, anyway. I suspect that, like the fishermen, they were also handsomely compensated.

Not too long after that, I heard a truly surprising story—that Sanzo of Kameya and the mistress of the Chidori had once been married to each other in a different town. I was standing in our garden when I accidentally overheard my mother, who was drinking tea with some neighboring wives, gossiping endlessly about it. It seemed a bizarre idea to me.

I suspect the story wasn't completely made up, because I later found out that neither Kame-san nor the mistress of the Chidori were originally from our town; both had come from somewhere else during the chaos immediately following the war, and had decided to stay.

I left town when I graduated from high school, and as a result I never again saw Kame-san. I heard, however, that the mistress of the Chidori thereafter opened a little eatery in the bustling town of Sakaemachi in the Chiba area, and that Kame-san had again vanished from that town as well. If it were true that Kame-san had been hanging around Sakaemachi, it may have meant that once he was indeed married to her. And although there was no way to tell who had been running away from whom, or who was following whom, it certainly made me think that the two of them were permanently entangled in a highly unusual affair of the heart. Unfortunately, I have no idea what happened to them afterwards.

The souvenir horn from India made me suddenly recall these odd characters from my distant past, yet I eventually decided to give the horn to my son, Gaku. He didn't necessarily want it, but I forced him to accept. He was such an extraordinary slug-a-bed that I would often rouse him a couple of times only to have him immediately fall asleep again, so I decided to suspend the horn from the ceiling directly over his pillow. I planned to honk the thing with a loud BLAT-BLET and make him get up despite himself.

When I first tried this idea out it was an immediate success, for after seven or eight blasts he covered his ears and yelled, "Help! Stop! Stop!" He was utterly routed by my new weapon. But while I was away one day he untied the horn from its string and hid it somewhere. When I returned I thought it would be easy to find—it had been hidden by a little boy, after all—but I had no such luck: I couldn't locate it anywhere.

In frustration, I finally asked one day, "Hey, Gaku. Where'd you put that horn from India?"

He smirked, feigned innocence, and said, "What? What

horn are you talking about?"

"Hey, don't try and pull one over on me, Gaku," I said, half-angry and determined to make him confess. "I know you've hidden it somewhere."

He was surprisingly resistant to this approach, and wouldn't budge.

A couple of months went by, during which I couldn't conduct my morning offensive with the horn. I eventually forgot about using it to roust Gaku, and just wished I could have it back for sentimental reasons. I told him this, and he seemed to understand, for he tried to find it again, but for some reason had no success. In two months, I figured, he had probably forgotten where he had hidden it in the first place, so the two of us got serious and tried a few times to look for it together, again with no luck. It started worrying me, for I wanted to find it as soon as possible and display it on the bookshelf in my room.

I don't know if the rascal was serious or not, but soon afterwards he told me with a straight face: "I'm not sure, but maybe I put that horn in the can for non-burnables by mistake, and then it went out with the trash."

FOUR

Dandelion

It was a Sunday morning. I had spread the newspaper on top of the dining table and was reading the sports section when the doorbell rang. Usually our only visitors on Sunday morning were bill collectors for the newspaper or milk deliveries. My wife would have answered the door, but she had left early that morning to attend a national conference for preschool teachers in Tokyo.

Ding-Dong! The doorbell rang again. I glanced at the clock on top of the refrigerator. Five to nine. I knew bill collectors had a job to do, but there was something irritating about their coming so early on Sunday. I had only gotten up early because of my wife. Normally I would have been sound asleep. As it was, I was reading the newspaper and drinking tea, but I was still in my pajamas.

Ding-Dong! went the doorbell impatiently.

"I'm coming, God dammit!" I cursed under my breath. We kept the money for day-to-day household expenses in a red vinyl purse in the drawer under the kitchen cupboard; I fished it out, purposely put a scowl on my face, and walked toward the front door.

I flung the door open, expecting to see either the sallow-faced, mop-top teenager from the Asahi newspaper, or the sullen, potato-faced lout from Koiwai Dairy, waiting to collect his money. I was thus utterly unprepared for what I encountered.

Three little girls were standing there with very prim and proper expressions, each holding a tiny gift-wrapped box in her hand. The one in the middle had a pageboy haircut, and I knew I had seen her somewhere a couple of times before.

"Um, is Gaku home?" she asked in a surprisingly loud voice.

"Well, er, ah. . . ," I stammered, words failing me for a second. Our door stopper was broken, so I had to hold the doorknob with one hand to keep the door from slamming shut. "Um, Gaku's still asleep," I finally said.

"Well," she said, "would you kindly give him this, then?" Her enunciation was textbook-perfect.

The two girls on either side of her added:

"And mine, too."

"Mine, too."

Simultaneously, they all handed me their packages.

"Er, what's this?" I asked.

"Chocolates. Please give them to Gaku."

"Chocolates?"

"Yes."

I held the little boxes in my free hand, feeling a bit bewildered. And then I remembered. Suddenly, finally, and all at once, it became clear. A-hah, I thought. A-hah. It was February 14. Valentine's Day. And three young girls had just brought my fourth-grade son a Valentine's gift of chocolates. I had recently heard on TV or someplace that, partly because of a highly effective advertising campaign by the candy industry, giving chocolates on Valentine's Day had become incredibly popular, even among elementary school children. But it had never occurred to me that my own son would be affected directly.

"Er, if you wouldn't mind possibly waiting here for just a second," I said, bemused by the politeness of the language I was suddenly slipping into, "I'll go wake up Gaku."

"It's really not necessary," the girl with the pageboy cut answered with a dead-serious expression. "If you could just give these to him, that'd be fine."

"Oh. I see. But, um, er. . . ." I was at a loss. It somehow didn't seem right to let them go away like that, not after they'd gone to all the trouble of bringing the presents over early on a Sunday morning. But even if I invited them in, the object of their interest was, after all, still sound asleep. I honestly didn't know what to do. All at once, I wondered if I should offer them some tea, or if we had any cake I could give them. If only, I thought, my wife was around to help me out.

While I was still pondering what to do, the three girls with no hesitation announced in bright, pretty voices: "Goodbye!" Then they bowed—one, two, and three—turned, and started to run out through our gate.

All I could only think of was to mutter a banal "Thank you" as I watched them dash off. Then I slowly closed the door. My left hand still held three variously shaped little boxes of chocolate.

"Oh, boy," I groaned for no particular reason. Suddenly, my own befuddled behavior seemed rather comical. I had become embarrassed and flustered just because three young females had handed me out-of-the-blue what were recently being called "love chocolates." The girls, I guessed, were the same age as Gaku—under ten.

"I'll be damned," I muttered, climbing the stairs to the second floor and not entirely clear what I felt "damned" about.

I threw open the rain shutters in my son's room to let in some fresh air and yelled, "Hey!"

"Hey!" I continued yelling as I yanked off his futon quilt. "What time do you think it is? It's time to wake up, that's what! It's morning!" His pajama top had nearly come off, leaving his midriff completely exposed, but true to form he never twitched, even when I pulled off his covers. The rascal was dead to the world, as usual.

"Hey! Wake up! Something big has come up! This is no time to stick out your bare belly!"

I grabbed both of his legs, scissored them, and flopped his body over so that he was face down. Then I twisted his legs across each other in an "X" and yanked him into the position known in professional wrestling as the "Indian Death Lock." This was something I often had to resort to. It was the only way to get the sluggard up.

"Hey! Rise and shine!" I yelled. "No breakfast for you unless you get up right now!" I held his legs firmly with my left hand, grabbed his head with my free hand, and pulled it backwards. It was rough treatment, but I knew it was the only way to get results.

"Oww! Stop! Dammit! Oww!" Gaku groaned and bleated pitifully, twisting his head desperately left and right.

"Up! Up and at 'em!" I said. "Something big's happened! Something really big!" I eased up on the offensive, and told him he had suddenly been favored with some very sweet gifts.

"Okay! Okay! Now let me go!" he said.

"Chocolates!" I said. "Chocolates from three young girls!"

"Okay! Okay!" he said, "I'm happy, okay?" Then, sensing I had let my guard down for a second, the little devil broke the hold I had on his legs and dove back under the futon mattress. I had no idea whether he actually understood what I had told him, or whether he was just responding instinctively. He was so cool and blasé about the whole business that it irritated me; all he wanted to do was squirrel back under the covers and continue sleeping.

I gave up, put the three boxes of chocolate near his pillow, placed the futon quilt I had just pulled off him out of reach, and with a final yell yanked off the mat he had hidden under. Then I left the room. I knew he would curl up like an armadillo and go back to sleep—until he finally noticed it was freezing cold and began griping.

That evening my wife came home exhausted from her conference. I announced that I had some extremely important news and immediately told her about the gifts Gaku had received.

"I can hardly believe it," I said. "Seems like we just toilet-trained him yesterday, and now he's already getting 'love chocolates.' And from three girls at once. Geez, I get chocolates once in a while in my line of work, but never anything like this."

"Ah," my wife answered, "but Valentine's Day isn't that big a deal for young kids today. It doesn't mean they're in love or anything."

I could tell the idea nonetheless tickled her, for she brightened up as she spoke. "I wonder who those girls were?" she mused.

"Well, I tell you, they were cute, sharp, and knew what they were doing. All three. I'm pretty sure I know one of them from his preschool days."

"I wonder if it was little Makie? You know, from the Ishihara-ras'."

"I don't know. But I tell you, my impression of Gaku sure changed today. He can't study worth beans, but he's awfully popular with the girls."

54

"There's something about him they like."

"At his age, the most popular boys are usually the best students or the best fighters. One or the other."

I could understand Gaku's popularity if it was related to his fighting ability. After all, he had a good track record on that score, and had already been reprimanded several times by his teachers. He had quite a reputation as a trouble-maker at school.

"Where's Gaku now?" my wife asked.

"Upstairs in my room, watching TV," I said.

"Hmm. I think I'll go take a look at something."

"At what?"

"At who sent the chocolates," she said.

Earlier in the day, I had casually asked Gaku who had brought the chocolates, and his curt reply had been, "How should I know? I didn't see anyone." The idea of searching for names somewhere in the wrapping papers had occurred to me, but it didn't seem a very manly thing for a father to do. Besides, by noon my initial excitement over the whole business had waned, and it no longer seemed like the sort of thing a parent should make a fuss over.

As it turned out, Gaku had torn the wrappings off the three boxes of chocolates and tossed them into his desk drawer.

"Why, look!" my wife exclaimed. "This one's from Tae Kawanishi, that little girl in his class! Remember? He talks about her a lot. He always says, "Kawanishi-boo. She gets on my nerves! She always bugs me about stuff!" She's the little girl who's always trying to take care of him. We should probably thank her, to tell you the truth."

Come to think of it, when we were in the bath Gaku had often mentioned a Kawanishi-boo. Usually it was in the form of a boast about how many times he had made her cry that day.

"From what Gaku says, you'd think all he ever does is tease her," my wife said, clearly enjoying all this immensely, "but to tell you the truth she's a lot smarter than he is. Apparently whenever he's up to his usual tricks, she really puts him in his place. That's probably why she gets on his nerves. At his age, the girls are always way ahead of the boys."

"Oh," she continued, "this one's from a Yatsushima. They've been in the same class ever since first grade. And look . . . here we are, one's from Makie, just as I thought. Makie Ishihara. I sort of guessed as much. She was in his class at preschool."

"I see," I said. "So that was the bigger girl with the pageboy hair cut. Thought I'd seen her before somewhere."

"Hmm," my wife said to herself, "so Makie came by, eh?" She stared at the words, written in ballpoint pen on the inside of the lid of a tiny, three-centimeter-square box: "Let's keep studying hard. Makie." From her expression I could tell she was tickled pink.

"Who'd you say that girl was again?" I asked.

"Remember when Gaku was in preschool and cracked up his teachers during that Christmas party? When he suddenly yelled, "I love Makie!"? That girl. They were in the same class until second grade."

"Oh, that girl!" I said.

Despite his tender years, our son had already caused many "mini-incidents," but his Christmas party "yell" took the prize for being both adorable and odd. I had been on a long trip overseas, so I only learned the details on my return, but apparently without warning he had suddenly stood up in the middle of the party and yelled, "I love Makie more than anybody in the whole world!" To call this grand proclamation an "incident" was inflating its significance, because that was all he did, but the spontaneity of it had made him the talk of the party.

When I first heard this story, I had been relaxing at home with my first drink of saké in a long time, and I recalled a similarly embarrassing incident from my own childhood. It was the sort of episode that family members always brought up when they got together every few years and the conversation turned to me. It was my "I wanna marry that girl!" incident.

I was born in Tokyo, but during my childhood my family lived for a while in a place called Shisui in the hills of Chiba Prefecture. We weren't there long. It may have been only three months or six months, I don't remember. To this day, I can't even recall exactly why our stay was so short, or why we were there. It probably had something to do with my father's work, but for some mysterious reason this subject was always off-limits in our family. I suppose I could ask now, but so much time has gone by it would somehow seem awkward, and as a result I'm still in the dark about it. All I know is that suddenly to leave a fairly large house with a stone wall around it in Setagaya for a place in the sticks in Chiba must have meant that something highly unusual was going on in my family. But that's another story.

We left Shisui when I was still six for a town closer to Tokyo called Makuhari, yet my father seemed to have lost the will to live, for he passed away shortly thereafter. I continued living in Makuhari until I was nineteen. Thinking back on it, we must have moved to Shisui right around my sixth birthday. I was, in retrospect, the same age as Gaku when he yelled in preschool that he "loved Makie."

There was a big concrete water tank next to the front gate of our house in Shisui, and it had a white tile embedded on the front with the words, "In case of fire." Next to the tank was a large maple tree, and I used to climb up it, rest a foot on the top of the tank, and watch the comings and goings from my perch.

To get to our house from Shisui Station, you had to climb a steep hill covered with drooping pines, where people claimed there were wild animals and sometimes even highway robbers. The war had ended only five or six years earlier, and except for an occasional truck hauling livestock or hay, climbing the hill with its engine wheezing and coughing like an old woman in distress, hardly anyone ever passed in front of our house. To someone like me, who had come from a bustling area in Tokyo, the rural scenery was a dreary, monotonous, and vaguely unsettling other world.

One day a horse-drawn cart came up the hill, looking stunningly colorful. In it was a young bride, dressed in a kimono with a sash around her waist made of gold-brocaded damask. Her wedding outfit was a type common immediately after the war, and though the colors were bright, the actual outergarment and the sash itself were probably rather cheap. But to me, used to seeing only a gravel road and a pine forest, she looked breathtaking.

I was riveted by the sight of her. With one foot on the water tank next to our gate and a firm grip on the maple tree, I watched as the cart slowly disappeared from view. "Wow!" I marveled out loud. "She's so beautiful, so beautiful." After that I was seized by a strange impulse, and I dashed inside our house, went into our large, eight-tatami-mat room and pulled all the sliding paper doors shut around me. I plopped down in the middle of the room and began yelling in a near-hysterical state, "I wanna marry that girl! I wanna marry that girl!" When my mother and older brothers came into the room to see what was going on, I began crying all the harder, and desperately tried to drive them away. Then I wailed even more.

My older brothers still tease me about this "I wanna marry that girl!" episode. My situation had been different from Gaku's when he proclaimed his love for Makie at his preschool party, but after hearing his story, and feeling the saké flow gently through my veins, I couldn't help suspecting there was a vaguely disturbing bond between the two of us.

"Well," I asked my wife. "Does Gaku still like Makie?"

"Hmm. It's hard to tell," she said. "I never really pursued the matter with him after the Christmas party."

It occurred to me then that Gaku had probably said he loved Makie in much the same spirit that he might say he loved popsicles and TV cartoon characters. "Most of the time he runs around with his belly bare," I said, "yelling about being hungry. I can't imagine him giving a damn about girls yet."

"But it looks like Gaku's 'proclamation' had an effect," my wife commented, putting the boxes of chocolates back in the desk drawer, "because Makie has apparently decided she really likes him. Her mother told me that the other day, with a laugh."

"Yeah. Girls are a lot more mature than boys at this age."

"Yes, and Makie's mother and father both seem to be enjoying what's going on with those two."

"Really?" I said. "That's interesting." Because of parent meetings at the preschool, I had met Makie's parents more often than I had met the girl herself. The mother, a stenographer, was a slender, refined woman of considerable beauty; her husband apparently worked at City Hall and was studying for a law exam on the side. Both of them were young, easygoing, and pleasant.

That night, while taking our bath together before dinner, I asked Gaku, "Hey, Gaku. Nice getting those chocolates today, eh? Don't eat them all at once."

"I know, I know," he said. Then, as some shockingly big bubbles began bursting on the surface of the hot water, he added with a happy look, "Oops, I think I farted."

"Who'd you get 'em from?"

"What? Oh, from Kawanishi-boo and some others."

"They all kids in your class?"

"Some're from other classes."

"Such as?"

"Such as Makie."

"She's the girl who was in preschool with you, right?"

"Yeah."

"You make sure you remember to thank everyone who gave them to you, okay?"

"Really? Do I have to?"

"Sure you do. They brought those chocolates all the way here just for you, so you have to thank them."

"How am I supposed to thank them?"

"Well, it would be nice to write 'thanks' or something on a postcard."

"What a pain in the neck!"

"It's an even bigger pain in the neck for them to buy chocolates for you and bring them all the way here on a Sunday morning."

"You ever get any Valentine's chocolates, Pa?"

"Sure, lots more than you. But mine are all work-related."

"Whaddya mean 'work-related'?"

"I write books for a living, right? Sometimes readers send me chocolates out of appreciation. That's what I mean by work-related. But I write everyone a thank-you card. Sometimes I write twenty or thirty."

"Wow! No kidding? Okay, I'll write, but it sure seems weird."

"What seems weird?"

Gaku fell silent for a second. I was soaping myself outside of the tub, and he got out and sat in front of me. He shook his head back and forth, and said loudly, "Boy, I sure am thirsty."

"What seems weird, Gaku?"

"Well," he said, "for example, I don't see why somebody like Kawanishi-boo would bring me chocolates. I know she hates my guts."

"Why should she hate you?"

"Just because. She always criticizes me."

I laughed out loud. I couldn't help it. I was sure Kawanishi-boo was a very mature little girl who was a mother-hen type (exactly the type who made devoted wives). Women like that tend to start fussing over men at a very young age. When Gaku referred to "Kawanishi-boo," I knew the "boo" part had been specially coined by him and his friends for people they regarded as a pain in the neck. All his slightly strict teachers were referred to with the "boo." He sometimes even called my wife "Ma-boo."

"What do you think about Makie?" I knew it was a little abrupt, but I asked anyway.

"What do you mean, 'what do I think of her'?"

I knew Gaku's somewhat irritated answer meant that he hadn't grasped the true significance of my question.

"Well, I mean about whether she hates you or not," I said.

"Why should she hate me? Makie's in 4-C, and, besides, we hardly ever talk anyway."

I felt as though I had asked a truly stupid question. I didn't say anything for a minute, and merely rinsed the soap off my body and stood up. "Let's soak one more time and get out," I said. "Then it'll be a cold beer for me."

"And it'll be a glass of cold milk for me," Gaku said, mimicking me. He stood up, dashed water over his head with great zest, and rinsed the soap off his body.

It happened about ten days after that. I returned late one night from a day-trip to Osaka. My wife greeted me with a broad grin, as if she had hardly been able to wait for me, and then she spread three postcards out on our kitchen table for me to look at.

The cards were somewhere between naive and primitive, and had been cut out of drawing paper with scissors. The confused jumble of jumbo and pygmy pencil marks adorning them was instantly recognizable as Gaku's incredibly bad handwriting. I looked at the addresses, and immediately knew he had finally gotten around to writing his thank-you notes for the Valentine's Day presents.

"Guess what?" my wife said. "For some reason Gaku suddenly remembered today, and he came up to me after dinner and said, "Gimme three postcards, Ma." Since I didn't have any on hand, I told him to make his own."

"Makes sense," I said.

"He was afraid the post office wouldn't deliver them, but I told him they will, as long as he puts stamps on them."

"Sounds good."

My wife had whipped up some indescribably gooey gruel to warm me up, and while sipping this hot, slightly sweet, mysterious food, I took a closer look at one of the thank-you cards Gaku had improvised. When I saw that he hadn't addressed it to "Kawanishi-boo," but that he had laboriously and correctly written, "Miss Tae Kawanishi," I couldn't help chuckling. On the other side, he had scrawled all over in his jumbo-pygmy characters, "Thanks for the chocs. They tasted great."

"This is pretty funny," I said, feeling warm and happy. I'd had a tiring day, having to go all the way to Osaka and back, and that morning I had woken up feeling as if I were coming down with a cold; I was exhausted. To make matters worse, it had been snowing since morning and that had created chaos at Haneda airport, delaying my plane's arrival by two hours.

"You know what?" my wife said, sipping from her own bowl. Then she deliberately and mysteriously lowered her voice to announce, "I heard something pretty interesting today."

"What?"

"I ran into Makie's mother this evening at the supermarket in front of the train station, and she told me that she and her husband were both born and raised in this town. Even better, she said they were classmates in the same elementary school here."

"That couple we know were?"

"That's right."

"A marriage between classmate sweethearts? No kidding?"

"That's right. Come to think of it, they always did seem more like pals than your normal married couple." My wife's eyes sparkled mischievously when she said this, as if she wanted to tell me more. "Take a look at all the cards," she added.

"Okay," I replied. I picked up the second one, which was addressed to Miss Kyoko Yatsushima, and turned it over. Like the one for Kawanishi-boo, Gaku had written in the same jumbo-pygmy script, "Thanks for the chocs. They tasted great."

"He seems to have a problem saying anything very profound, doesn't he?" I said, looking at my wife's face. She laughed and slowly shook her head back and forth for some mysterious reason.

Then I turned over the third card, addressed to Miss Makie Ishihara.

"What's this?" I said.

I looked at my wife's face again. She stopped shaking her head, and, as if she had been dying to point it out all along, began quickly nodding.

"This kid's not shy, is he?" I said.

On the back of the card to Makie Ishihara, just as on the others, he had written, "Thanks for the chocs. They tasted great." But there was one difference. Right in the middle of this one he had drawn a little flower. It was executed with a yellow crayon in the same crude style with which he scrawled the pencil characters. It consisted of a bunch of looping, round petals and could have been interpreted as a sunflower, a dandelion, or even a cosmos.

I laughed over the card, feeling better and better. "I wonder what kind of flower this is?" I said. "It's yellow, so I guess it must be a dandelion."

"I think you're right," my wife said. "It's small and yellow, so it's probably a dandelion."

"Yup," I said. "I'm sure this is his version of a dandelion."

I drank the last drops of gruel in the bottom of my bowl, laid the three postcards out on the table top, and pored over them once more. And then, for some reason, a faint memory washed over me of the young bride I had seen in the mountains of Shisui, dressed in a kimono with a sash of gold-brocaded damask, being jostled in her horse-drawn cart. Her image, and that of Gaku's funny dandelion crossed paths fuzzily somewhere deep in my mind, but that day I was too tired to pursue the notion any further.

The Live Bait Strategy

My fifth-grade son lies sprawled in front of me, a slumbering idiot with his mouth gaping open. A sixty-watt fluorescent light hangs directly above him in the middle of our tiny four-and-a-half-tatami-mat room. Its glare should be disturbing, yet he is snoozing away completely oblivious of it. Until thirty minutes ago, I had been lying on a futon mattress beside him in a strange semiconscious state between asleep and awake.

From a room on the other side of the hall, the bong of an old grandfather clock tells me it is exactly midnight. My body sends an earnest appeal to the core of my psyche: *If you don't start writing today, you're really going to be in serious trouble.* Simultaneously, I'm nearly overwhelmed by a terribly powerful, perverse force with the opposite message: *Hey, take it easy. You've had three beers today, and your body's tired from all the exercise* you had. Relax, forget it, go to sleep. You can always jump out of bed at four in the morning and start work right away. No problem. No problem.

As I'm engaged in this fierce spiritual tug-of-war between going back to sleep and working, I hear giggling coming from the room diagonally across from ours; it becomes a terribly vulgar external stimulus. From another direction, the sound of a fat man snoring assaults the nerves at the back of my brain; he sounds like a concrete mixer. Finally, with a grunt of determination, I manage to rouse myself.

Before my eyes, my silly son suddenly yells, "I did it!" twists around in a semicircle on top of his futon quilt, laughs, "Heh heh heh," and then falls silent again. I am sure that he's dreaming about fishing. He sounds like he's having a good time, even when he talks in his sleep.

We are staying at a bed and breakfast called Sazanami, near the port of Miike on the island of Miyake. We came here right after Gaku's summer vacation began, intending to stay five nights and six days, and today is the third day of our vacation. The owner of the inn had recommended that I take Gaku fishing for an ocean fish commonly found around here, the brown-striped mackerel scad. Following his advice we had left early in the morning and spent the whole day casting for scad from a breakwater near a small village.

The owner of the inn, Naganosuke Tamashiro, was from Okinawa. Huge ink rubbings of kelp bass and yellowjack were prominently displayed above the inn's front entrance, and below them I had noticed the words, "Caught by. . . ," followed by his name. Our host, it appeared, was quite a character, and, when it came to fishing, quite a pro.

When we arrived at the breakwater recommended by our expert angler friend, there were already twenty people there, their rods swishing through the air in the early summer morning light. From the top of the breakwater we could see schools of fish darting back and forth in the sea.

"Wow! Look at that!" Gaku exclaimed. "I know I can land a few of those!"

If Gaku sounded like a serious fisherman, in a very real sense he was. When Tamashiro had first seen us lugging our big cooler and bags of fishing gear into his inn, he probably thought that I was a typical father taking his son along on a fishing trip, but he couldn't have been more wrong. It was the other way around. Gaku was taking me, and his main goal in coming to Miyake Island in his summer vacation was a go-for-broke try at surf fishing.

Gaku had become serious about fishing about a year earlier, when I took him to visit my friend Tomosuke Noda, a river adventurer who lived by Lake Kameyama in Chiba Prefecture. Noda had shown him how to fish for crucian carp, and when Gaku had tried his hand at it he had caught five. This had had a powerful effect on his young mind, for when we returned home he began asking me if we could go to the bookstore. Since he normally never set foot in such places, I wondered what was going on, and even if something might be wrong with him. But when we went to a store in the neighborhood, sure enough he picked out three books, and, in what was an extremely hard-sell tactic, implored me: "I never ever begged you to buy me a book before, Pa, but now I am!" All three books were introductions to fishing.

Every month thereafter, Gaku spent his entire allowance on fishing gear. He began going with his classmates to nearby ponds or to the nearby Tama River nearly every day, and coming back with carp, topmouth minnow, and regular minnow that he had caught. He told me that he put the fish in his school's rainwater tank, and that he and his pals were feeding them to keep them alive.

I was fascinated by this sudden mania for fishing that he had developed, for I had never seen him throw himself into anything so wholeheartedly before.

One day I was particularly amazed. I personally knew next to nothing about fishing and had never really been very interested in it, deciding a long time ago that it simply wasn't my cup of tea. But of all the various types of fish, catfish had always held a strange fascination for me. In fact, once I had even gone to a river deep in the mountains behind Istanbul to catch the largest European catfish. Ostensibly it had been related to some work I was doing, but there was also something about the incredibly absent-minded look on their faces that I just appealed to me.

I therefore joked to Gaku, "Hey, if you're going to the Tama River again, bring me back some catfish, okay?"

To my astonishment, he went out and brought back a catfish nearly forty centimeters long. When I asked him how he had caught it, he said that he had rigged his line to catch it based on what he had read in a book, and that he had searched for it according to where the book said the catfish would be. He cautioned me to take good care of the fish when he gave it to me, sounding like a veteran angler.

Although Gaku was a fifth grader, I suspect this was the first time he had ever looked something up in a book and learned on his own. As I mentioned earlier, my wife and I had never given him any of the preschool tutoring so common in Japanese homes, and we had intentionally enrolled him in school "as is." So from the day of his enrollment ceremony there was a big gap between him and his classmates. Most of them had already had lessons in reading, writing, and so forth drummed into their heads, whereas Gaku was still writing many of his characters backwards until the third grade. Perhaps because of this, he also developed a strict policy of only reading comic books. I frankly felt quite touched that this same lad had learned about fishing and where to catch catfish from a book, and then gone out and actually bagged one for me.

Thereafter Gaku's entire life began to revolve around fishing. It was all he ever thought about, even at school. He drew pictures of fishing and ways to tie bait in his Japanese-language and arithmetic notebooks, and when we occasionally bathed together it was our main topic of conversation. Soon his speech was littered with fishing terms I had never even heard of before. My wife didn't have a clue what he was talking about. She said that he looked so crestfallen when she obviously didn't understand that she had begun to feign comprehension and nod in agreement every once in a while.

One other incident also showed how obsessed my son had become with the world of fishing. Gaku is a good fighter, and in fifth grade he was apparently the strongest in his class. Nonetheless, I was shocked when he suddenly announced one day in the bath, "You know what? I took on three sixth graders today."

As it turned out, it had been three sixth graders against three fifth graders—Gaku and his fishing pals, To-chan and Kamata. The fight had started, he said, when the sixth graders messed things up by throwing sand and rocks in the water tank where he and his pals kept the fish they had caught.

I got hot under the collar listening to this story. "Well?" I demanded in a manner unbecoming to a parent. "What happened? I hope you showed them a thing or two!"

"Yeah," he said. "First Keiichi came at me with a punch, so To-chan and me kicked him. 'N then [his way of saying 'and then'] Masaki, that coward, he kicked us from behind."

"Hmmm," I said, feeling genuine anger toward the sixth grader named Masaki. "Then what'd you do?"

"Then the class bell rang. We were fighting during the third-period recess."

"Oh," I said.

"We stopped when the bell rang," he continued. "Now they've really got it in for us." He made a face like his favorite professional wrestler when he said this.

How very like elementary school children, I thought with amusement, to stop fighting when the bell for the next class rang.

I later told my wife about the fight, saying, "Our boy's possessed by fishing."

"Well, that's okay, I guess," she replied, adding in a like-son-like-mother way. "It would seem kind of weird if he'd fallen in love with arithmetic or Japanese-language class."

Once Gaku had decided to become "Gaku the angler," he set his sights high: he was determined to try his hand at surf fishing, which was depicted in extremely attractive terms in his books, and to catch some striped jack, yellowtail amberjack, and striped beakperch at Point Satado on Miyake Island—the mecca for hard-core fishermen.

I had a vague idea what striped beakperch looked like, but frankly I had never even heard of striped jack or yellowtail amberjack. To make matters worse, at bath time Gaku started to interrogate me about what number leader was best for rigging a line for striped jack, and whether we could get hold of some bait for yellowtail amberjack, and so forth. I went out and bought an introductory book on saltwater fishing for adults and tried to bone up as fast as I could. I discovered that the three types of fish he was always talking about were prized by serious surf fishermen, and hardly what a fifth grader could possibly expect to catch the first time.

Gaku nonetheless withdrew his life savings from the bank in anticipation of our fishing trip. Two weeks in advance, following a detailed plan he made, he began buying super-heavy No. 17 leader for yellowtail amberjack, some wire line for striped beakperch, and some fishhooks so enormous they looked as though they should be attached to a crane.

The day before we left, I took one look at the enormous bag of tackle that he lugged over to me and winced. There's no getting around it, I thought, this is what people mean when they talk about "boyhood dreams." I must confess, though, that when I was around Gaku's age I, too, had always been obsessed by and pursued some sort of dream, so it wasn't as though I couldn't understand how he felt.

Before we departed, I assumed a serious expression and told Gaku: "Listen, there's something I want you to promise me. I read in a book that the people fishing for striped beakperch and greater amberjack at Point Satado are real veterans, and that it's extremely difficult and probably pretty dangerous. I know I don't know as much about fishing as you do, but I want you to promise me that when we get to the island we'll ask an expert's advice, and then we'll do as he says. Okay?"

When we arrived on Miyake, Gaku was initially disappointed because Naganosuke Tamashiro, our "expert angler," recommended that we go for scad, a smaller fish. But I told him we ought to at least give it a try, and he understood. And both of us thus went scad fishing for the first time.

The region had been covered with lava from a recent volcanic eruption, but the breakwater was considerably west of the affected area. Next to the breakwater, the scad flashed through the water in schools of one to two hundred, like a barrage of missiles. They were clearly far more vigorous than the other schools of little fish.

Since Gaku—now an ardent scholar of anything related to fishing—had read that scad often came to Miyake this time of year, he had brought along the appropriate tackle. For a style of fishing called "jigging," he had rigged around ten hooks at regular intervals on his line. Each hook was encased in thin rubber, making it an artificial bait. Above the hooks was a tiny net bag, or chum bag, in which he put a clump of groundbait of little krill that he had bought at a local bait shop. The idea was that each time the rod was swung or "jigged," a little bit of the krill would fall out of the bag to attract the fish. When they approached, they would be caught by the artificial bait on the line—the hooks—and then pulled in. In fishing parlance, this was called "chumming."

Interestingly enough, when we tried this it worked quite well. And since we were dealing with some very spirited scad, they fought hard when hooked, their silver bellies flashing in the light as we pulled them out of the water. It was truly exciting.

"Attaboy! Attaboy! Here we go!" Gaku said. It was his first attempt at this type of fishing, but he deftly pulled in fish after fish. I even caught a few with my rod. Sometimes two or three fish were hooked at the same time, and that really made us feel like experts.

Two hours later our compact cooler was filled with fish, and we were out of bait, too.

"I think it's time to call it quits, Gaku," I said, feeling eminently satisfied in the intense Miyake sunlight. "We'll never be able to eat this many. Let's take them back to the inn and have the owner make us a huge plate of mackerel sashimi. Man, it'll taste good."

Gaku seemed to be pondering something: "Um," he said.

"What's the matter?" I asked. "Look at all the fish we've caught. This is enough, isn't it? They're all big ones, too."

"Yeah," he suddenly said, "but do you think maybe we could take two or three of 'em alive over to Point Satado?"

"Point Satado? Why?" I asked.

"Well, see," he said, "live scad make the best bait for yellowtail amberjack."

"They do?"

"Right. I read it in a book. But the amberjack never come to the breakwater here. And there's a sheer thirty-meter cliff at Point Satado, so we can't use the chumming style of fishing like we do here."

"I see."

"That's why we ought to take some of these live scad along with us." He said this with a terribly adult expression, staring at the scad we had caught that were now stiffening in the ice of our cooler.

It occurred to me that Tamashiro might know what to do if we asked him; he might know either how to carry our scad to the point alive, or how to obtain even better bait to catch the yellowtail amberjack with. But this was the first time that either Gaku or I had ever attempted surf fishing, and I would have felt a little embarrassed telling Tamashiro what we really wanted to do, even if I were half joking. That he was an expert angler didn't make matters any easier.

"Hmm, yeah," I said, pretending to think hard. "I wonder if there isn't some way to do it." I was really trying to think of a way to get Gaku to give up his crazy idea and be content with catching smaller fry.

Gaku started taking apart his rod and reel, and said, "The fish'll die if we keep them in the cooler with the ice, so why don't we fill it with seawater, put in two or three fish, and then take them to the point as fast as possible by car?"

I had just been thinking the same thing. It was the only thing I could think of. But it also seemed terribly amateurish.

"Hey, it might work better than we think," Gaku said, trying to win me over. "Let's give it a try." His expression finally returned to normal, and he looked like a typical innocent fifth grader with a crew cut.

What are we doing? I thought. We could try Gaku's idea, but neither of us had any experience surf fishing. Our chance of actually catching any yellowtail amberjack was less than one in ten, and more like zero.

"Hang on a minute, Gaku," I said. "It's hot, so let's go get a bowl of shaved ice at one of those stores over there while we think this over for minute."

I set off, dragging our heavy scad-filled cooler, and started thinking about something else—something I often think about of late—which my friend Tomosuke Noda had said when we were at Lake Kameyama in Chiba Prefecture.

After casting a fishing net out with a grunt, Noda had said, "So Gaku hasn't rejected you yet, eh?"

In Noda's opinion, parents think they have to care for their children forever, but the kids usually create their own world and are gone before the parents realize it. A lot of parents around him, he claimed, had already been rejected by their children. To prove his point, he told me about his photographer friend Hideaki Sato, who had recently been rejected by his daughter, and he provided some photographic evidence.

The photographs showed Sato and his daughter before she rejected him and then a year later, afterwards. I realize that some people might doubt whether such changes in a relationship are really marked enough to be visible in a photograph, but I have to admit that Noda seemed to be correct, for in the photos he showed me the daughter was clearly becoming psychologically independent of her father and starting to go her own way.

"So did Sato let it get him down?" I asked.

"Yeah, he took it pretty hard at first," Noda replied.

I knew Hideaki Sato well myself, so I could almost see the situation in my mind's eye, and there was something funny about it. But after hearing Noda's story, I began to wonder when Gaku would start distancing himself from me. It seemed hard to believe at first, but from what Noda said, I would probably be roundly rejected before I realized what was actually happening. It was—I decided in an unusually objective frame of mind—a very plausible scenario after all.

Gaku finished wolfing down his bowl of strawberry shaved ice and asked with a dejected look, "Well? Come up with any good ideas yet?"

"Uh, no, I'm still thinking, Gaku," I said.

"Hurry up so we can go catch some yellowtail amberjack, Pa. People'll laugh at us if we tell them we went all the way to Miyake Island and didn't even try to catch any."

"Uh, right," I said. I was clearly losing out to this young boy who had nothing but fishing on the brain twenty-four hours a day.

"I know," I announced. "We'll implement the strategy I mentioned earlier—transportation by taxi."

"What's 'transportation' mean?"

"It means to carry things from one place to another."

"Oh."

Gaku and I continued our serious discussion for a while longer and then, after determining the best time to catch the fish, decided to put our plan into action the next morning. In other words, we would get up at five, go to the breakwater at Ako, spend thirty minutes catching a few scad, put them in a cooler of seawater, and rush them to Point Satado.

I was reluctant to divulge our strategy to Naganosuke Tamashiro, so I decided just to ask him to take us to the breakwater in the morning; from there we would get a taxi by ourselves.

The next morning my alarm clock woke me at ten to five. The guest in the room next to me had been up till the wee hours of the morning, and as usual his snoring sounded like a concrete mixer. In the evenings he was always glued to the phone at the entrance of the inn, making call after call and talking interminably in a low voice, so perhaps he was some sort of salesman who specialized in making the rounds of the island. There was also a group of four young women staying in the inn, but all they ever seemed to do was head for the beach in front of the inn and swim all day.

I woke Gaku with a "Hey, we're going fishing! It's the yellowtail amberjack strategy!" and he immediately jumped out of bed. Considering that he normally never even twitched when I yelled at him in the morning on a schoolday, he was remarkably alert.

We threw the box lunches we had ordered the night before in our packs and quickly left the inn. After commenting that it would be even hotter than the day before, Naganosuke Tamashiro lent me a straw hat. "If you catch a lot of scad today," he added, scratching the gray stubble of beard that stood out on his dark skin, "I'll make you some salted mackerel."

It was still early when we arrived at the Ako breakwater, and, sure enough, there were only five or six fishermen there. All of them were fishing for brownstriped mackerel scad, using the jigging method. Since we had tried it the day before, we let our lines play out right away, scattering the groundbait. In less than two minutes, I caught a scad. Then Gaku did, too.

"Okay," I said, "let's each pull in one more, and then go."

He nodded silently.

We soon had four fish for live bait. We carefully pulled the hooks out of them so as not to hurt them and put them in our cooler, which we filled with seawater. Then we quickly packed up our tackle and hurried to a public phone booth at the harbor to call a taxi. I was afraid the other fishermen on the breakwater would wonder why we had come so early, only to leave after catching a couple of fish, but they were so absorbed in their fishing that they never even glanced at us.

When I had inquired the night before, I had been told that if we called a taxi it could get us to Point Satado in three minutes. At that hour of the morning, of course, there was probably no one else on the whole island who wanted a taxi.

Sure enough, the taxi came. On the way to Point Satado, Gaku kept his ears pricked for any sounds coming from the trunk. He seemed to fear that our cooler might tip over, but I assured him there was no chance of that happening. I was more worried that our four scad friends, so suddenly confined to a small cooler, might decide to give up the ghost. It had just occurred to me that we should have put only one fish in the cooler, but I knew it was too late to worry about that.

Our frizzy-haired driver parked on the road in front of the lighthouse at the point and muttered with a somewhat disinterested expression, "You going after greater amberjack? Or opaleye?"

"Er, well, sort of," I said.

Having come this far, there was no turning back. We had to charge ahead at full speed.

We pulled the cooler out of the taxicab trunk, and Gaku said, "Let's take a look and see how they are."

"No," I said, restraining him, "Let's just hustle over to our fishing spot as fast as we can."

Gaku nodded in agreement.

We hurriedly climbed the path lined with bamboo leaves and orange seaside day lilies until we reached an opening in the trees. In the early morning sunlight we suddenly saw an awesome expanse of blue ocean. Point Satado was like a snout, shoved rudely against the Pacific Ocean, and we were on top of it. The fishing area was below the lighthouse, and it was a sheer cliff nearly thirty meters above the surface of the sea.

"Wow, there's hardly anyone here yet," Gaku said, his voice quavering slightly.

On top of huge boulders protruding here and there we could see four or five fishermen casting with their rods. For a second I thought they were all using live scad for bait to catch yellowtail amberjack, but on closer inspection this did not appear to be the case. At Point Satado, the really serious anglers were not limiting themselves to yellowtail amberjack; they were going after all sorts of big fish.

I felt myself getting excited for some reason. I quickly scanned the point, looking for the least dangerous-looking outcrop. After choosing what seemed to be the most stable boulder, I lowered the heavy cooler from my shoulder. Gaku immediately lifted the lid. The seawater inside was a muddy blue-black, and two scad were floating on the surface, white bellies up. Another one was twisting his torso feebly and holding his head at a weird angle. But, miraculously, at the bottom there was one survivor apparently still breathing normally.

"We did it!" I announced into the brisk morning sea breeze. "Our live bait strategy worked!"

"Yeah. We did it, huh," Gaku said. He was wasting no time, and had already begun to quickly and carefully extend his casting rod and attach his spinning reel.

"You know how to put the bait on?" I knew it was a silly question, but I asked it anyway. It was our first time with live bait, so everything, including putting on the bait, was a new experience for Gaku.

"It says in my book that we should pin the hooks on their backs," Gaku announced, suddenly serious in his expression and tone. This was the big chance he had been waiting for, and I could tell he was a little tense.

The "pinning" he had learned about in his book consisted of crudely jamming a fat hook into an area above the fish gills, and running it toward the head. It felt like some sort of ritual we were performing before finally taking on the really big fish. The scad was weakened, but when we stuck the hook in above the gills it must have hurt, for it flapped its tail vigorously in Gaku's hands.

"Here we go," Gaku said.

I took a look at the sea I was about to cast into. It was much farther below than I had imagined. The rough waters of the Pacific became huge swells and smashed into the giant boulders at the base of the cliff, creating a huge eddy of white foam that then spread out across the sea. Given the number of huge waves crashing in and then disappearing, I was surprised that the noise was not louder; from our perch high up on the huge boulders, it sounded more like the roar of a distant ocean. I reasoned that it was either because we were so high above the sea, or because the ocean wind was so strong it was carrying the sound away before it reached us. I couldn't tell which it was.

Gaku stood on top of our crag, and, with a slow but surprisingly deft motion, cast his specially rigged line with the live bait far out into the surf. Thick yellow No. 17 line played out from his spinning reel with a whish, singing faintly in the strong wind off the ocean.

Gaku's go-for-broke attempt at surf fishing resulted in defeat; he never got to pull in a single fish. On his first cast, the live bait was either eaten by fish, torn apart by the shock of the toss, or scraped off by rocks; when he reeled in, the scad had vanished from the hook. We then attached our second, nearly dead scad to the line and cast it out; then we cast with the corpses of the third and fourth, all to no avail.

Gaku seemed unaffected by our failure. In fact, he was in a far more upbeat mood than I expected. That night, after triple helpings of greater amberjack sashimi prepared by Naganosuke Tamashiro, he announced with a satisfied look, "Well, I guess surf fishing's kinda difficult. But the ocean's a lot more fun to fish in because it's a lot bigger than some old stream."

"Well, maybe you're right, there, Gaku," I said, "but remember that this was your first time. Next time you'll have better luck." From the start, I had been pessimistic about our chances, but it was odd, because like Gaku I felt somehow satisfied, despite the failure of our "live bait strategy."

I was feeling the effects of three beers when I told Gaku, "We'll give it everything we've got next time."

But suddenly I secretly wondered if I would be rejected before the next time came around.

SIX

The Eagle and The Pig

My friend Tomosuke Noda had come back from Canada. From the sound of his voice on the other end of the phone, I could tell he was low on energy.

"Man, is it ever hot here!" he groaned. "I can hardly stand it!"

Japan's steamy summer heat was getting him down, and no wonder. He had left on June 27 to spend fifty days kayaking down the Yukon River in Canada, where he said fall was already in full swing and it was chilly sleeping in a tent. We, on the other hand, were experiencing record high temperatures, and for the last sixteen nights it had been positively tropical.

"Why don't you come over for a cold beer?" I suggested.

"Good idea," he replied. "But just thinking about going over to your place makes me perspire. I'm going straight to the Japan Alps instead."

"What about the plans for Hokkaido?" It was August, Gaku's summer vacation was almost over, and Noda was supposed to take him to Hokkaido and spend the week of the twenty-fifth to the thirty-first kayaking down the Kushiro River.

"Yeah, well," he said, a little life returning to his voice for the first time, "it's so hot I'm thinking of leaving a couple of days early. I'll let you know as soon as I get the tickets."

"You mean you might leave on the twenty-second or - third?"

"Right. I wanna go as soon as possible. Tell Gaku, okay? Tell him to get ready to fish."

"Seems like that's all the kid's been doing every day—boning up on fishing. He told me, by the way, that if you called I should ask what kind of fish are biting in the Kushiro this time of year."

"Hmm, well," Noda said, "probably white spotted char and salmon trout right now. You'd better tell him to bring some feather jigs and gang rigs when he comes."

Noda said he was going to visit the manager of a lodge called the Donkey House at the foot of the mountains. From this I assumed he would be staying at the lodge, but when I asked, he said no, he wouldn't feel right about that. He was going to pitch his tent in the front yard and camp out. "I'll just borrow their bathroom," he said.

I laughed. It was a very Noda type of thing to say.

"Anyway," he said before hanging up, "I'll let you know as soon as I set the date for Hokkaido."

With that he left for the Japan Alps.

The Tokyo heat didn't affect me the way it did Noda. I had just returned from a much hotter place—right below the equator in the Maldives, smack in the middle of the Indian Ocean. Still, I had several jobs that had to be finished, and I felt a little beat myself.

I had taken one of the jobs as a lark, after a magazine editor

I knew made an offer that was hard to refuse.

"Want to try your hand at making fifty thousand yen's worth of art?" he had asked in a deadpan voice.

"'Fifty thousand yen's worth of art?'" I answered. "What are you talking about?"

As it turned out, his magazine was going to celebrate its fourth year of publication that fall, and to commemorate this the editors had decided to ask fifty people associated with it from the beginning to create works of art for under fifty thousand yen. In principle, the subject matter could be anything as long as it fell into the category of "art." The finished works would be exhibited at a Shibuya department store and auctioned off on the spot.

"A little art might help you forget the heat," my earnest editor friend said. "Why not try it?"

By coincidence, for the last four or five years I had toyed with the idea of carving an eagle from a large block of wood, so I told him, "I'll accept, as long as you don't mind a carving."

"A carving," he said in a flat, official-sounding voice. "That'll be fine. What kind of materials do you need?" I felt as if I were talking to a pencil pusher at City Hall.

"Well," I replied, "I'll need a piece of wood thirty centimeters by thirty centimeters by one meter long, and it has to be soft enough to carve."

"I understand," he said. "I'll try to locate something for you right away."

Then he hung up.

I forgot all about this conversation until the beginning of August, when the same editor called to say he had located the wood for me. He said he would meet me at the do-it-yourself store from which he had ordered it when I came to pick it up.

"We've already gone way over budget," he said apologetically when I arrived.

In my ignorance, I had assumed the wood might cost ten or

twenty thousand yen, but to my shock it had cost ninety thousand.* I suddenly felt extremely nervous. It was such expensive wood. Could I really create "art" out it? I had casually specified what size the block of wood should be, but with it right in front of me, it seemed far larger than I had imagined. It was enormous—magnificent and solid, yet there was something elegant about it. When we asked the salesperson what type of wood it was, he replied that it was katsura, and that it was ideal for carving. As I stared at it, I couldn't help feeling that it was far too fine for a rank amateur like me to mutilate with a chisel and that I really should stick with the tiny woodblocks I carved every year to print my New Year's greeting cards.

"Don't worry about going over budget, Mr. Shiina," the editor said. "We just want you to do the best work you can."

I didn't know what to say, but I knew he was trying to encourage me. He even bought me some of the beautiful chisels professionals use.

When I took everything home, Gaku immediately came up to me with a happy grin. He was already bored with his summer vacation.

"Hey, Pa," he said, "what are you going to do with that?"

"Carve something," I answered, trying to look and act as much like an artist as possible. "A big eagle."

"No kidding?" he said. "You sure you can carve such a big piece of wood?"

"Sure. I'll just whittle away at it. Then I'm going to title it 'The Black Eagle' and display it at a department store."

"No kidding? But you might ruin it. Why don't you just leave the block standing like it is, and call it 'The Empire State Building' instead?"

"You and your goddamn wisecracks," I said in a tone unbe-

*About $700

coming to an artist. To tell the truth, I was impressed. Gaku had expressed my own sentiments exactly.

As it turned out, I didn't do anything immediately. Before I could figure out how on earth to carve an eagle out of my huge block of wood, I wound up going to the Indian Ocean, to the Maldives. After I returned, and before I knew it, we were halfway through Gaku's summer vacation. But according to a message from the editor, the work had to be completed and delivered to the department store by September 4.

Shortly before Noda returned from Canada, I realized I had to get serious about my creation, so under a scorching hot sun I began whittling away at the block of wood. When I had first picked it up, the salesperson had drawn himself up and assured me with considerable pride that the wood was "extremely fine grain, and therefore no problem to work with." Sure enough, he was right. The chisel blade cut into it smoothly. It was so much fun to work with, in fact, that although I began wielding my saw and chisels in the early morning to avoid the heat, I often wound up working until noon. And the more my creation assumed the vague contours of a giant monster bird, the more interesting the work became, so much so that I started putting aside the other work I had to do and concentrating on the carving. I found it infinitely more satisfying to go out on the veranda, wield my chisels, and work up a sweat in the sweltering heat than to labor at some boring writing job.

In what soon became a daily ritual, Gaku began coming home from swimming at the school pool and poking fun at my creation.

"Ha ha ha! You call that an eagle? Looks more like a parrot to me!"

"It doesn't look like an eagle now, Gaku," I replied, feeling generous as I sweated profusely, "because I haven't carved the beak yet. Just wait."

"Hmph. Really? I think you oughta stop where you are now, and just title it 'The Parrot.'"

While hurling this sort of abuse at me, Gaku picked up a chunk of wood I had cut off the block of katsura, and, when I wasn't using the saw and chisels, began creating something of his own.

"What are you making?" I asked.

Very seriously, the rascal replied, "It's a secret."

Noda sounded much better when he called from the mountains. He said they were going to leave for Hokkaido on August 24, and that a Canadian friend was going to join them. The three of them would all run the river together.

Two days before their departure, Noda came over to my place. It was still terribly hot in Tokyo, but we were finally going to have a drink to celebrate his safe return from the Yukon. Before leaving for Canada he had seemed a tad overweight; now he was shockingly thin.

"Looks like you lost a little paunch," I said.

"Yeah," he replied. "Didn't have a drop of liquor for two months, and there was hardly a damn thing to eat, either. We had to sponge food off the Indians."

"You didn't catch any fish?"

"Well, we caught some one-meter-long king salmon, but we couldn't get hold of any rifles this time, so we never had any meat. The biscuits were great, though. I thought they were the best thing I'd ever eaten in the whole wide world, so I brought a bunch back to Japan with me. But you know what? Here, they taste like the worst thing in the whole wide world."

I wondered if I had made an error of judgment. I had assumed Noda would have gorged himself on meat in a place like Canada, so my wife and I had mainly prepared draft beer and lots of sushi rolls. I also knew he had once said something about, "only shitting every three days" if he ate too much meat. Sure enough, when a dish of steamed pork did appear, he hardly touched it.

I had experienced the same problem as Noda on long trips overseas, and it usually put me in a foul mood. I was actually supposed to leave for a three-month trip myself that fall, traveling through Australia and Siberia and returning to Japan in February. I knew Australia would be no problem, but I had heard that Siberia was bitterly cold at that time of year—that it got down anywhere from minus fifty to an extreme of minus seventy degrees centigrade. One of the directors I knew from the TBS TV station, who had been there on a scouting trip in May, had even told me that absolutely no vegetables were available, and when he had asked for some fruit he had been given two or three measly slices of cucumber. Apparently the local people ate mostly venison and beef. As I listened to Noda, it occurred to me that I, too, was soon going to be crapping only once every three days.

"Do you think the Kushiro River's safe?" my wife asked.

"Sure," Noda answered. "Don't worry about Gaku. He'll be fine, 'cause I trained him on the Naka River rapids. The Explorers Club of some university recently made a big deal about their 'grand adventure' running the Kushiro, but it'll be a piece of cake for Gaku. He may, in fact, be the first fifth grader in all Japan to run it."

Gaku laughed. At first I thought he was laughing because of Noda's comment, but then I looked again and saw he was just laughing at a TV show that happened to be on.

The next day we had to pack Gaku's rucksack for his river trip. He was going to be living in a tent for a week, so he needed quite a few things, but they had to be kept to a minimum since everything had to fit into a tiny kayak. His fishing gear alone took up most of the space. He was truly looking forward to fishing on the river.

"Take only the absolute essentials, Gaku," I said. "You know what 'absolute essentials' means, right?"

"Yeah," he replied. "Sort of. Noda says there aren't going to be any bait and tackle shops along the river this time, though."

"That's why you've got to take only what's absolutely essential."

"Okay, okay, I hear you."

An hour later Gaku's rucksack was crammed so full of stuff he couldn't get the top closed. We took everything out once more and checked it against the list Noda had provided, but he had followed the list faithfully and there was little to eliminate.

"Hmm," I muttered. "This won't do, and we can't very well have you take two rucksacks."

"Well, heck," he responded, "in that case I'll just cut down on my clothes. I packed five pairs of underwear, but I can get by with two. And I only need one pair of sweat pants."

"Now wait a minute, Gaku," I said. "Don't forget you're going to get wet a lot."

"Who cares?" he replied. "If I get wet, I'll just wash 'em. After all, I know how to do the laundry, Pa."

On the surface, what Gaku said sort of made sense, but in reality he wasn't giving me logical answers. He was desperately trying to figure out some way to avoid reducing all the fishing gear in his pack.

"Okay," I said. "If that's the way it's going to be, we'll have to take something out and tie it on the outside of your rucksack."

We took out his sleeping bag and crammed the canteen and mess kit, which had been sticking out, back inside. Then we tied his sleeping bag to the top of the rucksack with an elastic cord. When he shouldered his pack, the bag stuck way out, and he resembled a sorry-looking recruit in the old Imperial Army.

"There we go," I said. "That oughta do it."

"There's only one thing I'm worried about, Pa."

"What?"

"You know that medicine you put on when you get bitten by bugs? I know I don't have any room, but I'd really like to take some with me."

"Hmm," I said. "Well, maybe we'll have to consider that, then."

In the afternoon, after finishing with Gaku's bag, I returned to our sun-scorched veranda and resumed work on my creation. I had nearly finished the basic shape of the eagle, so the next step was to start on details like the beak and talons. It was odd, but having gotten this far, I was becoming obsessed with my carving.

The night before, the phone had rung while I was chiseling the outline of the eagle's talons.

I picked up the receiver and heard a gravely and mysteriously self-important voice suddenly ask, "Who is this?"

It seemed an awfully rude way for a caller to announce himself. It would have felt wonderful to retort, "Who the hell do you think you are? Why don't you try telling me who you are first?" But it was too late. I made the pitiful, moronic, and typical telephone response: "Uh, er," I stammered.

"You're Shiina, right?" the voice said. "Listen, this is Funatsu. What the hell do you think you're doing? What's all that hammering?"

Funatsu was our elderly next-door neighbor. He always sounded as though he were interrogating people.

"Er, I'm carving something," I muttered.

"Where's your common sense, man? What time do you think it is? And by the way, I don't know whether you're doing judo or whatever, but you're always making a racket at your place. Try being a little more considerate of others!"

"Uh, yessir, er, I'm sorry if we. . . ."

Before I could finish my sentence he had hung up. I looked

at my watch. Nine-thirty. It seemed awfully early to make such a fuss about noise, but it was true I had been completely engrossed in what I was doing, and the sound of my mallet hitting the chisel must have been fairly loud. The racket from the "judo or whatever" that he had referred to was from the pro wrestling matches Gaku and I often held. In the summer we always left the windows open, and Funatsu apparently heard everything. But if he had just stuck his head out his window and yelled, "Shut up!" we would have gotten the message. Something about the way he had gone to the trouble to call didn't sit well with me. This old man always seemed to have some gripe against us.

The phone call that night upset me so much that the next morning I became even more absorbed in crafting my eagle's talons.

Gaku came over and started working on his piece of wood, too.

"Gaku," I asked again, "what on earth are you whittling?"

"It's a secret, but you really wanna know? I'm carving your face."

"Hmm," I replied. "Well then, just make sure I look good, okay?"

"Yeah. That's not easy, though."

"And don't cut your fingers off, okay?"

"Don't worry."

The kid continued sitting in the corner of the veranda with his back to me, banging away furiously at a chisel, refusing to show me what he was making.

The flight to Kushiro was scheduled to depart from Haneda airport at nine-forty in the morning, and since there was quite a lot of luggage, as well as kayaks for three people, we had agreed to meet Noda there at eight-thirty. That meant we had to leave the house by six-thirty. Which meant that I had to wake Gaku up at five-thirty.

A week ago, complaining of the heat, Gaku had moved his mattress to our wooden-floored room and started sleeping there. He didn't seem to sleep very soundly, for every morning I would find he had rolled off his mattress and was sprawled somewhere on the floor with his belly exposed. In the summer his school participated in the calisthenics program that was broadcast daily on national radio at six-thirty, but, true to form, he had never once opened his eyes and made it to school in time to join in. At first my wife tried to wake him up, but no matter how hard she shook him, he never twitched, so she eventually gave up. Gaku totally flunked morning calisthenics.

On the day Gaku was to leave for Hokkaido, it irritated me to see him suddenly transformed into an eager beaver. As I suspected, all I had to say was, "It's five-thirty! Up and at 'em!" and lightly shake his shoulder. He was up in a flash. He washed his face in no time flat, took his normal pre-breakfast crap, and sat down at the dining table. As soon as he finished, I knew he would take yet another crap.

After making sure Gaku had everything, we left the house at six-thirty. I knew it was going to be a hot day again because the sunlight was already intense.

"I bet you're in seventh heaven, Gaku," I said, stating the obvious as we walked. In the morning light, his boyish face was positively beaming. "Just don't forget you're going to run a river that's one hundred and fifty kilometers long, and that there are several places that are dangerous even for grownups. You be careful, okay?"

"Don't worry," Gaku said, slightly irritated. I couldn't tell if it was because of the difficulty of keeping his balance with the load on his back, but he was walking with a slight forward stoop, again looking like a raw recruit in the army.

We arrived at our rendezvous spot thirty minutes early, but Noda came exactly when he had said he would. He had seven huge pieces of luggage, including a pair of two-man kayaks that weighed twenty kilograms, a one-man kayak for Gaku that weighed fifteen kilograms, a tent, and assorted cooking utensils. The Canadian who would accompany them was apparently going to join them in Hokkaido a day later. We had to pay an extra thirty thousand yen because the baggage was oversize. The official at the airline counter knocked sixteen kilograms off the total weight of sixty-six, but he was a stickler for red tape and wouldn't budge beyond that, carefully collecting every single yen of the fee.

"It's a damn shame," Noda muttered. "But that's the breaks. Let's go grab a bite to eat. You guys haven't eaten yet, have you?"

"Gaku has, but not me," I answered.

We went up to the restaurant on the second floor of the airport and quickly ordered the "B" breakfast on the menu. It arrived at our table in no time flat, and it was a truly picture-perfect example of a "B" grade breakfast. It consisted of a tiny piece of salmon and a razor-thin slice of seaweed.

"Well," I said, "the more I think about the two of you spending a week on the river, the more I wish I could go along. After this I have to go home and dedicate myself to my art work again in the heat."

"Yeah," Noda said, "I've got to admit I'm looking forward to this trip down the Kushiro as much as Gaku is. On the Yukon, you can paddle for ten days and the scenery never changes, but on Japanese rivers it changes with nearly every stroke."

While Noda and I talked, Gaku ate some strawberry ice cream and listened quietly.

"This'll be my third time down the Kushiro," Noda continued. "The last time some of the people living along the river helped me out a lot. They were kind enough to give me eggs and stuff like that, so I hope I meet them again."

"That's nice to hear."

"You know what, though? I recently heard that some college kid tried to run the Kushiro last month, but the rapids were too much for him, so he gave up, abandoned his kayak and went home. We might find a kayak somewhere."

Gaku laughed, but it only made me feel uneasy. The Kushiro River was the Kushiro River, and Noda had just reminded me that its rapids could make an adult give up and go home. I knew Noda himself had run rivers all over the world, but I was Gaku's father and I couldn't help feeling a little worried about him.

Perhaps Noda sensed my thoughts, for next he said, "But don't worry. I've been down it twice and I know the rough spots like the back of my hand. And besides, I've got my camera, so if Gaku flips over I'll get a great picture of him."

Gaku laughed again.

Then the airport loudspeakers announced that All Nippon Airways Flight 741 to Kushiro was boarding.

"Well," I said, "I guess it's time to go."

We all stood up, and then I realized that Gaku hadn't gone to the bathroom after breakfast that morning. "Don't you have to take another crap?" I asked him. Turning to Noda, I added, "This kid always shits twice in the morning, before and after breakfast."

"Uh, oh," Gaku said with a sudden realization. "That's right. I only went once."

Noda chuckled. "You're a healthy lad, Gaku!" he said. "Today you get to do it in an airplane. It'll be a flying turd, for a change!"

Gaku laughed.

Earlier, while waiting for Noda in the lobby, I had bought some insect repellent spray for Gaku at a kiosk. I suddenly remembered and handed it to him.

"Don't put too much of this stuff on," I advised.

"Don't worry," he said.

I watched Noda and Gaku until they cleared the metal detector, and then I quickly left the area. Gaku's first big adventure was about to begin.

I got on the monorail at the airport, planning to go straight home and resume my carving, but when I got off at Hamamatsucho Station it was too hot and humid, so I changed my mind. I hadn't had much sleep for the last few days, and my arms and shoulders felt heavy and stiff from all the hammering and chiseling I'd been doing. I took a short subway ride to my office, turned on the air conditioner, and stretched out on the sofa. I must have been asleep an hour or so when the phone rang.

It was my friend Hitoshi Sawano, the illustrator. In a slow, drawling fashion, he explained that he'd just come back from a long trip and was just calling to say "Hi." But then he seemed to remember what he really wanted to say, for his speech suddenly speeded up and he asked, "By the way, how's the wood carving going? I know you said you were going to carve an eagle, but like I mentioned before, you really ought to make it an alligator. There are too many carvings of eagles around. Yeah, an alligator. It should definitely be an alligator."

I knew Sawano was going to enter something in the "art exhibition" himself. I had also heard from my very serious editor friend that he was going to be a little sneaky and enter a chair that he had actually made ages ago, when he had been nuts about woodworking.

"Well," I said out of spite, pretending not to know. "What about you? You got anything yet?"

His answer was evasive: "Yeah, sort of, but it's incredibly hot these days."

Then he added, "Hey, in September, why don't we go diving off Hachijo Island? Last week when I went to west Izu it was just exquisite under water. It made me want to spend my whole life there."

After this incredibly affected statement, Sawano hung up, and the phone immediately rang again. It was a salesman from the Tokyo Credit Association.

"Would you be interested in making any other deposits, sir?" a polite male voice announced.

"No," I said. I just wanted to sleep some more.

It was early evening when I finally returned home. My wife's summer vacation had started that day, and she had gone to a lodge in the mountains to pick wildflowers, so I was all alone. I mulled over the possibilities. Maybe, I thought, I should go out for a drink and have dinner with Sawano and his pals in Shin-juku, but it was already too late for that. Going out again to eat seemed like more trouble than it was worth. I had my eagle to carve, but I also had a lot of writing that I had let slide while I was occupied with my art. It was almost dark, and if I started carving away, I'd probably lose all track of time and work until late at night-and be chewed out by my crusty neighbor again.

I opened the refrigerator and took out some smoked cheese and three cans of Budweiser. Then I took them up to my room on the second floor. I took my time drinking the beer, and just as it started to get dark, I heard the sound of drums. At first they seemed so loud I thought they must be coming from close by, but then I realized they were from an All Souls' festival some distance away. I listened carefully, and mixed in with what had first sounded like just drums, I could faintly hear the folk songs that always accompany the festival dances. It seemed awfully late in the season for such a festival, but that made me all the more determined not to lose track of the sound.

I walked out onto the veranda with my beer in hand. A little square hunk of wood lay on the ground in the farthermost corner. I knew that Gaku, in imitation of me, had been carving something of his own, and I knew right away that this was it.

When I had asked him before what he was carving, he had said, "Your face, Pa." I wondered how far he had gotten with his carving, and what it looked like, so I went over and picked it up. It was still only crudely shaped, and I couldn't figure out where the top or the bottom was supposed to be, but as I slowly rotated it in my hand and stared at it, I saw some faint pencil lines. Apparently they were drawn as a guide to the areas he was planning to cut away.

I took a second look, and realized he had drawn a pig with an extremely long snout. The goddamn rascal, I thought.

And then, for a second, I laughed all by myself, just like Gaku: "Ha ha ha."

SEVEN

Thirty Years

G aku was coming back from the Kushiro River. Thinking he would arrive at Haneda airport with Tomosuke Noda, kayaks, pup tents, and a ton of luggage, I was waiting in the lobby, ready to act as a porter. But he appeared accompanied only by a very serious-looking female employee of All Nippon Airways. It was a bit of a letdown.

"Are you the father?" the woman asked in the stern tone of an elementary school teacher. I automatically tensed, wondering what had happened, but she apparently had nothing particular to report. She unfolded a paper in her left hand, handed me a ballpoint pen, and said, "Sign here, please." It was some sort of release form for minors.

"You came back alone?" I asked Gaku.

"Yeah," he said. "The tents and sleeping bags got all wet, so Mr. Noda said he was going to dry them out before he left."

I signed the release form. The airline woman smiled an official little smile, and then quickly returned in the direction she had come from.

"Well?" I asked Gaku as we walked down the stairs leading to the monorail station platform. "Did you have fun?"

"Yeah," he said. "I caught a rainbow trout about sixty centimeters long. And I caught more salmon trout and dace than we knew what to do with."

"I bet it was little chilly, wasn't it?"

"It was freezing."

A week after Gaku and Noda had left for Kushiro on August 24, I still hadn't heard a word from them, and I had started to worry a bit. It wasn't that I was especially afraid something would happen to Gaku because he was running a river with Noda; it was just that I hadn't heard anything.

Finally a phone call had come.

"We're fine," Noda said in his usual gruff, deep voice.

"Good," I said. "How's it been going?"

I was surprised how loud my voice sounded. The funny thing about talking long distance on the phone was that, although I had no problem hearing Noda, I raised my voice more than necessary just because I knew he was calling from the hills of Hokkaido.

"Well, it's been a lot colder than I expected," he said.

"Gaku hasn't capsized?"

"Nope. He's doing great. The foreigner kept flipping over all the time, though, and he ruined one of the kayaks. I'm taking the day off to dry out our tents."

The "foreigner" was the Canadian who had gone along on the trip; a magazine editor who, at 6 feet seven inches and 220 pounds, had the physique of a professional wrestler.

"So anyway," Noda continued, "the foreigner decided to go back to Tokyo early. Gaku and I want to do things right, though, so we'll probably be back in early September. No problem with Gaku's school, right?"

"Uh, no," I said, imagining a big burly Canadian sinking pathetically in the rapids, "that should be okay. Has Gaku been doing as he's told?"

"Gaku? Sure, we'd be lost without him. He's been catching dinner for us every day. You want to talk to him?"

I heard Gaku's voice, always low for a young boy, come on the phone. "That you, Pa?" he said.

"Yes. You having fun, Gaku?"

"Yeah."

"What sort of things have you been eating every day?"

"Fish and noodles and stuff like that."

"You come home in one piece, okay?"

"Okay."

There were many things I wanted to ask him, yet when we actually started talking I couldn't find much to say. I knew he would have lots of stories, but they could wait until he returned.

"You take care, Gaku," I said, "and you pay attention to what Mr. Noda tells you, okay?"

"Okay," he replied.

That had been the extent of our phone conversation, so when I finally met Gaku at Haneda airport, I still had little idea how his river trip had really gone.

"School starts tomorrow," I said, "so we'll have to cut your hair when we get home."

Normally, Gaku's head was shaved, but since I hadn't run my clippers over it once during summer vacation, tufts of hair were sprouting from beneath his baseball cap and covering his ears. When he had left on his trip, with his sleeping bag lashed to his rucksack at a crazy angle, he had looked like a hapless army recruit; now he looked more like one of the ragged urchins that roamed the streets of Japanese cities at the end of the war. But I noticed that when I mentioned the need for a haircut, he made a face.

"We don't really have to do it today, Pa," he said.

"Yes, we do," I insisted. "We'll do it today. Otherwise you'll look like a street urchin."

"Who cares if I look like a 'straight erchin.' "

"You know what a street urchin is?"

We stood on the monorail platform, and Gaku looked up at me with an unhappy expression and said, "No, but it's probably somebody weird, right?"

While Gaku had been kayaking down the Kushiro, I had spent a lot of time at home, alone. I went for days without speaking to anyone, working alternately on my eagle carving in the heat, or on the full-length novel I was writing, I had no idea how well I was doing with either.

Late at night, when it came time to shower and have a beer, I would automatically find myself wondering how Noda and Gaku were doing as they camped beside the Kushiro. I was convinced these were some of the most important, satisfying days Gaku would ever have. But I was also vaguely worried that his memories of the experience would fade and that he wouldn't be able to apply them to his life.

I often wonder how much a fifth grader retains of his experiences as he grows into adulthood. I think I know how much I have retained, but I feel uneasy when I think of myself at Gaku's age. My memory is perverse, and it crawls in and out of my mind like a worm. I hate the childhood self I remember, with a passion. I'm convinced I was an obnoxious brat.

When I was six years old, we moved from Tokyo and lived in a small fishing village in Chiba Prefecture. I was the kid from Tokyo. And this is where my unpleasant memories start to intervene.

When I went to school, my mother made me wear a beret. It

was navy blue, with a little pom-pom on top—the sort of thing little girls normally wear. And to make matters worse, although nearly all the boys in my class had crew cuts, the hair under my beret had been carefully cut in a horribly feminine style that only sissies affected.

My shaven-headed classmates all immediately gathered around me and my beret and began teasing me, yelling, "Pom-pom, mop-top!" The leader grabbed my beret, spun it around on his fingertip, and sent it sailing through the air. I stared, helpless. Another kid caught the beret, spun it around on his finger, and sent it soaring again. I'm not sure, but while my beret flew back and forth over my head, I think I merely plopped down on the ground in a confused, cowardly silence.

When I returned home I told my mother I was never going to wear the beret again. She made sad-dog eyes, and said, "What on earth's the matter with you, child?" or something to that effect.

My mother taught traditional Japanese dancing, and she liked fancy, fashionable things, but they were the last thing in the world I needed. It was the same thing when she made me take a special cushion to school for my chair; I knew I would be the only one in the whole class with one, so I resisted. But again, she made her sad-dog eyes and said, "What on earth's the matter with you, child?" or something to that effect. Unable to protest any more, I wound up taking the cushion she had made for me to school and hiding it in my desk.

Eventually the kid with the beret from Tokyo turned out to be a fairly good student and was appointed head of his class, which entitled him to tell his classmates things like, "Hey, I don't think you're supposed to be doing that," when they were up to some mischief. (Just recalling this makes me more convinced than ever that I really was an obnoxious brat.) But then, between fifth and sixth grade, the same kid finally became one of the boys, trading his mop-top hairdo for a crew cut, stealing persimmons and peaches, and throwing baseballs through windows like the rest of them.

It is around this time that flickering images of my father finally appear in my memories. I was the same age then as Gaku is now.

The big difference between my relationship with my father and Gaku's relationship with me is in our ages. Gaku and I are thirty years apart, whereas the age gap between my father and me was infinitely greater. It wasn't so unusual in those days, I suppose, but I was born to my father terribly late in his life. (I have never written about my own childhood before in this fashion, and I certainly did not intend to turn this essay into a confessional, but I am fascinated by the fact that, as I write, many things I never understood before are becoming absurdly clear).

I come from a family of ten or so children, not all of whom have the same mother. The story behind this is filled with dark, mysterious, and novel-like secrets, and I have always feared that opening the door to them might have unforeseeable consequences, so I have deliberately kept it shut. But for this same reason I have never really thought much about my father. He died when I was in sixth grade, and until the other day I had no idea exactly how old he was at the time. To be more honest, I may have known once, but I made no attempt to preserve the memory and thus forgot.

While writing this series, I called my eldest brother to ask, "I know this is rather sudden, but how old was Father when he died?"

"He was sixty-six," my brother answered. "Are you thinking of writing something about him?" His voice had a slight edge to it. I may have read too much into it, but I detected an implicit threat from the head of our family: Be careful what you write.

"No, not really," I replied. "I was just thinking of jotting down some recollections of him."

"Oh," my brother said. Then, like a soap opera actor reciting his lines, he changed his tone and added, "And by the way, how's little Gaku? Why don't you send him over to visit us once in a while? We've got lots of ripe persimmons on our tree this year." Then he hung up.

Hmm, I thought, so Father was sixty-six. I was strangely impressed. At sixty-six, he was old enough to have been my grandfather, let alone my father. That meant that when I was in fifth grade like Gaku, my father had been fifty-six years older than me.

One of my most vivid memories of my father is from a pub in the city of Funabashi. It was winter, and a year before he died, so I was exactly Gaku's age. During my fifth-grade summer vacation I had defied my mother and shorn off my mop-top, so I was sitting in the dusky reddish light of the pub with a crew cut.

"Eat your crab," he said.

I don't remember exactly why my father took me to the pub that day. He was drinking saké. A man born in the nineteenth century, he sported a beard and made his living as a certified public accountant. I can't remember anyone else sitting beside him in the pub, but I remember how noisy it was.

"Eat your crab," he said.

I was just a child, and I remember feeling excited and happy. I'm sure it was simply because I was in a pub (a terribly exciting, mysterious, and vaguely sinister place where grown-ups went) and because I had my father all to myself that day.

I have absolutely no recollection about how we got to the pub, or, for that matter, how we left. I just remember that our table was graced with the rhomboid shapes of several of the blue crabs that are caught in large quantities near Funabashi at that time of year, and that I sat across from Father silently eating them.

I have another, less pleasant memory of my father. It was some time after we ate the crab together, and I was probably a sixth grader. I was doing "airplane spins" with some pals in the junior high school grounds behind our house. This was an improvised acrobatic stunt that required one to stand on a high bar, and, while falling backwards and simultaneously grabbing the bar with both hands, to fly forward in an arc through the air.

While engaged in this feat I saw my father get off the bus that passed along the road in front of the schoolyard, and slowly walk toward us. His demeanor was always stern, and he wasn't the type to casually greet anyone with a big "Hi, there!" even if they were children, so I didn't say anything when I first saw him. Airplane spins took a certain amount of courage, though, and I thought I was pretty good at them, so I wanted to show him. To draw his attention I called out to my friends in an extra loud voice, "Ready or not, here I come!" or something like that.

I couldn't tell whether he noticed me or not. From atop the high bar I could see him hunched over like an old man in his heavy gray overcoat, silently continuing down the road without looking in my direction.

I kept playing "airplane" with my pals for a while longer, but then for some reason I failed to grab the bar with one of my hands. With my body bent at a weird angle, I crashed headfirst into the sandbox below the bars, and hit my head hard on the corner of its wooden edge. A sharp pain shot through my head, and when my friends helped prop me up, they suddenly started yelling something about an "emergency!" I had cut my head on the edge of the board, and was bleeding quite heavily.

My friends carried me home. My mother heard the commotion and dashed out into the yard in a panic, crying, "Oh, my God! What will we do?" When she saw my wound she called out for my father, saying, "Come quick, Dear! Makoto's been hurt badly!"

One of my older brothers rushed out of the house at full tilt, and when my mother told him to hurry and get my father, he dashed back inside.

But my father never came out. Instead, my brother came running back again and told my mother that Father had said that I "had had it coming, horsing around like that," and that they should "take me to a doctor right away." My brother looked at us with a strange expression, as if he didn't know what to do.

My brother and my friends carried me to the Maeda Clinic near the local train station, where I received five stitches for a crescent-shaped gash on the back of my skull.

"Well," the doctor told me and my mother, who stood next to me, "I think he'll be all right, but make sure he takes it easy for a while, because there's always a possibility that he could have a seizure later."

On the way home, my mother muttered over and over, "I just can't believe how heartless your Father is. He wouldn't even stop and look when he saw his own son injured."

I had tried hard to get my father to notice me on the high bar, and I thought that he had walked by without seeing me. It was a shock to realize that he had seen everything.

Gaku seemed to have grown in places after his ten-day river trip.

We stopped in a noodle shop in front of Kokubunji Station, and ordered what he and I always ate together around that time—fried dumplings, noodles, and rice. And then I finally asked my crew-cut boy, "Anything interesting happen?"

"Yeah," he said. "We took a hot bath by Lake Kussharo, and that was fun. You can only get there by kayak."

"You mean it was a natural thermal spring?"

"Yeah. A 'nacheral thurmal' spring. You mean like an out-door hot bath, right?"

"Right. I bet it felt great."

"We ate raw crayfish sashimi at Lake Kussharo, too. There's lots of crayfish there."

"No kidding? What about the current in the river, though, wasn't it awfully fast?"

"Yeah, it was pretty amazing. Mr. Tracy flipped over three times. When you flip over you get carried a long way by the river."

"What about you, Gaku? Didn't you flip over?"

"Naw. I'm good at it."

"Hey, don't make me laugh. I know it's really because you don't weigh so much."

"Yeah. Once Mr. Tracy sank with his kayak pointing straight up."

I laughed just like Gaku always laughs: "Ha ha ha."

"Did you like sleeping in a tent?" I asked.

"Yeah."

"What about the meals? Did they taste good? What did you eat?"

"Just like I told you on the phone. Fish and noodles."

"I'll bet Mr. Noda and Mr. Tracy drank saké, didn't they? What did you do then?"

"I read comic books."

"Inside the tent?"

"Yeah."

"You used the light from your headlamp?"

"Yeah."

"Then what did you do?"

"I went to sleep."

"No kidding," I said. With Gaku, conversations always tended to be fragmented.

The fried dumplings arrived. For a young boy, Gaku like to dip his dumplings in soy sauce with an enormous amount of spicy red chili oil mixed in. But that day he didn't even touch them with his chopsticks. He just kept staring in the direction of the kitchen, saying, "Man, I'm starved. I hope the noodles come soon."

"Why don't you go ahead and eat your fried dumplings first?" I suggested.

Gaku looked at me with an expression I couldn't recall seeing before, a strange sort of stare. "Naw," he said. "I'm gonna put the dumplings in the noodles and eat them. That's the way we always ate them when we were camping."

The noodles soon arrived, and Gaku put six dumplings on top of them, and began wolfing down his version of fried dumplings-noodles-and-rice. It seemed as though the boy had always been able to eat more than an adult. I have a pretty healthy appetite myself, but it had become increasingly difficult to hold my own against him; often he out-ate me.

"Oh, yeah, there was one other thing that was really interesting," Gaku said with his mouth stuffed full of rice. "The day before, when we were pitching the tent, there were lots of little holes in the ground. I wondered what they were but couldn't tell, and even Mr. Noda didn't know, so I just slept on top of them."

"So what were they?"

"I was really surprised when I woke up the next day. My tent was rocking back and forth, so I stepped outside, wondering what was going on, and found a whole bunch of cows all around. They were licking the tent all over."

"No kidding?"

"Yeah, Mr. Noda said there was a farm above us, and that we had pitched the tent in the place where the cows came to drink water."

"Really. That's a pretty good story."

"Yeah. And after that we visited the farm and I got to

107

drink a bunch of fresh milk."

"No kidding. I'll bet that tasted good."

"Yeah," Gaku said, with a very manly expression. "It was really super-duper good."

At one point in my life, I began to wonder if my father had actually been running away from something. I suspected this because of the way our family had suddenly uprooted itself and moved—it was almost as if we had fled from Tokyo to the countryside.

After we vacated our fairly large house in Tokyo's Setagaya Ward, we stayed for a brief period in the old part of Tokyo, and then soon moved to a rented house in the remote and rural town of Shisui, in Chiba Prefecture. We were only there a few months, though, before we settled in a small town on the Chiba coast.

My father—normally stern and unapproachable even to his own family—was finally able to relax and spend his days in peace in our new home. But then people from the tax office came with a warrant to seize all our household effects. They had a list of possessions to attach, and so that no one else would see, they pasted it inside the door of one of our wardrobes.

Later, my mother would often point to the list, make her sad-dog eyes, and say in a mournful voice to me and my next older brother, "A bad person took advantage of your father."

I don't know if the paper was still attached to the wardrobe door when I fell off the high bar and cut my head, but not too long after that my father died. For a tough man of his times his death seemed all too simple; he just snapped, like a string breaking.

I was in the kitchen when it happened. I heard a strange gasp from the direction of the guest room. It was my mother. I knew something was wrong, and I ran to her. My father, wearing his yukata robe, was lying face-up on top of his futon quilt, with his head bent back. My mother, kneeling beside his pillow, kept muttering over and over again as if she were chanting a mantra, "Quick! Call Nagai! Quick! Call Nagai!"

Nagai was the name of my father's doctor in the neighborhood. I dashed outside barefoot and ran all the way to Dr. Nagai's office in the fading evening light. A female physician with a porkish build and a quintuple chin, she made her way to our house in a fake sort of run, with her arms pumping back and forth and her legs scarcely moving at all. When we arrived, my father was already cold to the touch.

A funeral attended by many people was rather an enjoyable event to me as a child. I got to eat lots of delicious things, and I got to stay up late. I felt quite happy amid the milling crowd of assorted lively relatives.

Oddly, I have a vivid memory of my mother saying in front of our relatives, "Well, I have no regrets. When Father passed away, I was right there, and I closed his eyes and wet his lips like you're supposed to, but I did it with a final, farewell kiss. I'm satisfied."

At the time I was terribly confused and puzzled. How on earth, I thought, could my mother say such a creepy thing in front of others? But now I realize that my mother was a teacher of dance, a woman, and my father's second wife, and it was probably one of her last chances to assert herself. It's just a guess on my part, but I sometimes wonder if my father had actually been running away from "women."

After ten days of camping, Gaku and his possessions stank horribly. When he took off his cap, his sweaty head emitted a smell like a stale towel.

"Let's give you a haircut before you take a bath," I said.

He suddenly looked sullen and said, "No, I don't need one yet."

"What are you talking about, Gaku?" I said. "Your head smells like a stale towel."

He fell silent and just stared at me for a while. He looked so serious I couldn't help smiling.

"What's wrong with having your hair cut?" I asked.

With eyes cast downward, he answered in an unusually anemic voice: "I dunno, it's just that. . . ."

" 'Just that' what?" I persisted. He still looked downcast and troubled, but as I stared at the top of his shaggy noggin I finally realized what the problem was. Once before, in second grade, someone had teased him about being a "Baldy" and made him hate his haircut.

"Well," I had said then, "why don't you slug him? You're the toughest kid in second grade, aren't you?"

"But he's a 'firfth' grader, Pa," Gaku had replied in a muffled pouting voice.

"Well, in that case, heck, you ought to be able to handle him easily, right?"

I thought he meant a "first" grader, so there was something about his reluctance that I didn't understand at once. Then I realized that he had meant one of the older kids. He had really been trying to say a "fourth" grader.

Remembering this episode, I asked: "Gaku, do some older kids still make fun of your haircut?"

Gaku fell silent for a minute, then looked up at me and nodded weakly.

"Punch 'em. You're tougher than any sixth graders," I advised.

"I did once before. But they're a bunch of cowards, and three of 'em ganged up on me at once."

"Why not punch all three of them?"

"Well, it's easy for you to say that, Pa, but Fuji and them are pretty strong, too. They're sixth graders, you know."

110

"Don't you have any pals who'll stick up for you?"

"Maybe. When Mi-chan and To-chan come to school with new crew cuts, Fuji makes fun of them, too, so maybe they'd help me."

Mi-chan and To-chan were both pals of Gaku, in the same class and on the local baseball team.

"I think you and your pals ought to show Fuji and his gang a thing or two," I said. I grabbed my electric hair clippers off the shelf above the bathtub and sat Gaku down on the floor. "Here we go," I announced. "Shut your eyes."

Gaku closed his eyes and made a face that said: Damn, I hate this, but what can I do?

I had the clippers set to "extra short," and the blade roared merrily through the woolly new growth over his forehead.

Something about his sullen demeanor still bothered me, so I asked in a deliberately up-beat voice, "Do your pals Mi-chan and To-chan have their hair cut at home, too? Or do they go to a barbershop?"

"I dunno," he said in a still petulant tone. "I never asked."

When I shaved a broad swath straight back from his forehead, his head looked like the ridiculous before-and-after ads of balding men on television and in the newspapers. Normally, at this point, I would have shown him what he looked like in the mirror and we would both have had a laugh. That day, though, it somehow didn't seem appropriate.

I next shaved his temples, then spun him around, and shaved the luxurious growth of hair on the back of his head. He had a scar there from falling off a swing in preschool, and the two stitches he'd received had left a thin hairless line. Every time I saw it I thought about the old scar on my own head, from the time I had fallen off the high bar.

Well, I thought, I never did have the seizure the doctor at the Maeda Clinic had warned about. Thirty years had already gone by since then, and thirty years had also gone by since the death of my father. And this same thirty years also represented the difference in age between me and the son whose head I was just shaving. And beyond those thirty years, an image of myself, wearing a beret and being teased by my shaven-head classmates, flashed into my mind.

I turned to Gaku, whose head I had just finished shaving, and in an angry tone I suddenly gave him the same advice I had given him once before: "If Fuji and his gang make fun of you, Gaku, you punch 'em good, okay? Let 'em have it."

Gaku paused for a second, and then said in a low voice, "I will, Pa. I will."

EIGHT

Fishing for Mudsuckers

Gaku's love affair with fishing began when Tomosuke Noda, who knows everything from A to Z about rivers, had shown him how to catch carp. Gaku is like me, I suspect, in the sense that when something strikes his fancy, his involvement in it tends to be total.

One day my wife tiptoed over to me and with a shocked expression exclaimed, "Gaku's reading a book!"

I knew right away that it was about fishing—I had a pretty good idea of what was going on with him. I went to his room, trying to act as normally as possible. Sure enough, he was sprawled on his bed reading a book on fishing. It was a book for grown-ups, titled *How to Catch 'Em: An Introduction to Stream Fishing*, and since it was not the sort of book we normally had lying around the house, I knew he must have either borrowed it or bought it on his own. That alone was quite a surprise; as I have mentioned before, although a fifth grader, Gaku normally never cracked a book, and when forced to write book reports for school, he usually scraped by with illustrated story books meant for kindergartners. It was also the first time I had ever seen him reading in such an adult pose. There was something so hilarious about the sight, in fact, that I stood in the doorway and burst out laughing.

"Can you really read that?" I asked, smiling.

He glanced up from his book, and stared at me with something resembling a scowl. "Of course I can," he said.

"Well," I said, "is it interesting?"

"Yeah."

"It's about how to fish in streams?"

"Yeah."

His replies were so curt I didn't really know what to say, so I responded with a banality: "Well, that's good," I said. "Hope you learn a lot from it."

He mumbled something about having finally figured out how to tie on a bait ball gang rig, but when he glanced at me his expression really seemed to say, I heard you, so now leave me alone, okay?

Whenever Gaku went to Noda's place at Lake Kameyama he plunged deep into the world of fishing. With near-obsessive determination, he would stand fishing in one spot by the bank of the river until he caught something, and he apparently caught quite a lot. Reeling in a big fish also had an exponential effect on his enjoyment, driving him into a frenzy of excitement. Whenever he came back from the lake and told me what had happened that day, his cheeks would be flushed and the words would pour out of him.

He had had fishing on the brain for day and night for some time, and spent his entire monthly allowance of six-hundred yen on fishing tackle. After school, on days when he didn't have soccer practice, he and some pals from his class would go to what they called the "Tatchan Pond" near Lake Tama, or to the Tama River itself. Sometimes when I came home early and took a bath with him, our conversation would be almost entirely about fishing; I learned a lot about the sport in a hurry.

As I have described in an earlier chapter, nearly every time I saw Gaku, he told me he wanted to go saltwater fishing. He had already read a variety of books on fishing, and he had apparently decided that while stream fishing was okay, saltwater fishing would be even more fun because there were infinitely more fish in the ocean and many more interesting ways to catch them. And besides, he said, he really wanted to try to catch a yellowtail amberjack. I thought it was out of the question, because I knew that amberjack were extremely difficult, even for expert anglers. But I had been away from home so much that I had been unable to take him anywhere, so I finally decided to make his wish come true during his summer vacation.

After Gaku experienced surf fishing, the "wonderful world of fishing" hooked him body and soul. His room was littered with fishing gear, and anyone opening his door was immediately assaulted by a very fishy smell.

When I told Gaku one day that I was going to travel from Lake Biwa to Wakasa Bay with Noda as part of a job for a weekly magazine, he gave me an obviously despairing look. Then, fixing his gaze off to the side, he muttered, "Grown-ups get to have all the fun, don't they?"

" 'Fun'?" I said. "But Gaku, this is work."

"That's why I said grown-ups get to have all the fun. They get to go fishing for work."

"Listen, Gaku, I'm not just going to fish. I'll be pitching a tent and paddling a kayak on the lake. I have to write an article about it."

Unfortunately, that was the wrong thing to say. Gaku had

already kayaked down the Kushiro River with Noda that summer, so he knew how much fun it was.

"Tell you what," I said, 'when I come back, I'll take you somewhere."

"Okay, Pa," he answered, staring straight at me hard enough to burn a hole in the air. "But it's a promise, remember? And don't forget it's going to be the perfect season for ocean fishing."

I had not paddled a kayak with Noda in a long time. He had invited me to go on a river trip with him several times, but I had always been too busy, and as a result Gaku's skills had apparently surpassed mine.

"Yup," Noda said, as the prows of our kayaks sliced through the unusually shimmering waters of Lake Biwa, "he sure knows how to paddle."

We could see Chikubu Island ahead of us, covered in haze and looking like an upside-down bowl. The October wind on the lake felt good.

"Aroof-Aroof," Gaku barked. Gaku was the name of a scatterbrained pup that Noda had recently acquired. It had a jet-black snout like a bear's and was, he said, a one-month-old male. We had brought him in the car all the way from Chiba Prefecture and taken him with us in the kayaks. Noda lived alone, so if he had a pet and went anywhere, he either had to take it with him or leave it with a friend. Like me, he traveled a lot, so this was always a big problem.

"I hope you'll forgive me," Noda had said with an apologetic smile, "but when I first laid eyes on this pup he reminded me so much of Gaku that I knew there was only one name for him. See? Look at his face. Don't you think he looks like Gaku? He's got the same powerful legs, too. Both of them are going to grow up to be pretty big, I bet. And just like your son, this Gaku here always takes a shit before and after he eats. I was really impressed by the resemblance."

I laughed along with Noda.

"I always take him along with me on Lake Kameyama," Noda said. "I'm going to turn him into a first-rate canoe dog."

"Aroof-Aroof," Gaku howled mournfully again. As soon as we had pulled out from the shore, he had crawled atop the kayak, and, in an attempt to walk on the surface of the lake, had fallen into the water with a splash.

"After all the times we've been out in a kayak," Noda said, shaking his head, "this mutt still can't tell the difference between water and land. He tries to walk everywhere."

"Reminds me of my son, the way he's such a numbskull."

The canoe dog barked again: "Aroof-Aroof."

Noda fished a bottle of whiskey out from between his legs, took a slug, and asked, "So how's your Gaku, anyway?"

"My Gaku? Well, when I told him I was coming with you to Lake Biwa and to the sea off Fukui, he made a face and said something about grown-ups having all the fun."

"Sort of makes sense."

"He keeps bugging me to take him out to sea. Whenever he's not off stream-fishing with his pals, he's dog-fishing off our second-story veranda."

"Dog-fishing?"

"We've got this mongrel pooch at our place called Dai, see, and Gaku tries to snare him with a fish lure he made out of wood."

Noda stroked his mustache, beamed as if immensely pleased, and said, "Sounds just like Gaku."

"The mutt's is a bit of numbskull, too. It thinks the lure's a real fish and tries to eat it. Then Gaku starts cranking and reeling in his line, hauling the dog up and saying, Whoa! I've got a big one this time!' "

Noda laughed.

"They make quite a pair!" I said.

Noda and I pitched our tent on the northern shore of Lake Biwa and camped for a night, then moved to Wakasa Bay and camped another night. Little Gaku prowled around our campfire, ate a variety of left-over fish, and then curled up and went to sleep in a corner of the tent.

The next day, Noda had to go home early by train, and he asked me to take care of Gaku for a while. I put the pup in the car in a plastic shopping basket and drove home. When I arrived at our house, the human child Gaku was almost beside himself with curiosity.

"Hey!" he burst out. "Where'd you get that dog? Where'd you find him?"

"This," I announced, looking at the faces of both Gaku and Gaku, "is a dog called 'Gaku,' just like you. But he's probably one hundred times cleverer than you are."

My wife had been informed of the situation a moment earlier on the phone by Noda. She picked the puppy up, hugged him to her breast, and said with an absolutely straight face, "Why, he's even cuter than the real Gaku."

With the typical, dying-to-know expression of a child, Gaku asked, "Are we gonna keep him?"

"Only for a little while," I answered. "He's really Mr. Noda's dog."

"So *where* are we going to keep him?" Gaku asked.

"Probably inside the house," my wife said, yanking her head back with an "oops" as Gaku tried to lick her nose. "If we let him out in the yard, Dai'll jump all over him."

Our dog Dai lived in the backyard.

There had been a great deal of snow that winter, and in January it had covered the ground for five days. On the day when it snowed the hardest my wife found Dai barking and tethered to a telephone pole in front of her preschool. Over the phone she had said, "There's a pure white puppy dog whimpering in the snow. It looks so sad." Then she had asked if she could bring it home. She said it had a little wooden tag on its collar, with "My name is Lili," written on it.

Later, at home, she had turned the puppy over and discovered that it had a little peepee. Since a name like "Lili" sounded rather queer for a male dog, we decided to call him something else. My wife, having brought him home, immediately claimed parental naming rights, and thereafter declared him to be a masculine-sounding "Daigoro." Noda had given us two rabbits called Care and Ott at year-end, so Daigoro became the third member of our animal family. It had long white hair, and a face that looked as if it had been drawn by a cartoonist.

A month or so later, a carpenter who lives in the neighborhood and loves dogs came by, picked up Daigoro, and announced to us that the pup was in fact not a male but a fine female. What my wife had taken to be its peepee was apparently something altogether different.

With the dog now a female, it seemed a little cruel to call her Daigoro; in a delicate compromise we decided to just call her Dai, and write her name in phonetic script instead of with a more formal Chinese character. She was, therefore, a dog with a rather convoluted history.

The day Dai realized there was a junior member of her tribe living in the house, she began dashing around the yard, loudly reminding us of her existence. The puppy Gaku, for that matter, also seemed extremely interested in the white dog running about outside.

On the second day we decided to let Gaku out in the yard. And who should welcome it most but the human Gaku.

Gaku quickly extended his fishing pole from our second-floor veranda. He had a toy fish made out of wood tied to his line.

"I've got a bite! I've got a bite!" he said in a hoarse whisper in the direction of my room.

I looked, and sure enough the tip of his extra-strong surf-casting rod was straining badly and occasionally whipping back and forth through the air.

"This feels about like it did when I caught rainbow trout on the Kushiro," Gaku said with an expression of immense satisfaction. "Come to think of it, the black bass on Lake Kameyama felt sort of like this, too."

I looked out my window and saw the puppy below; he had the wooden fish between his teeth, and was violently shaking his head from side to side.

"So Gaku's fishing for Gaku, eh?" I said.

Gaku laughed with a strange low sound: "Heh heh heh heh."

Fall was well on its way, and the trip Australia I had planned was fast approaching. I was supposed to spend a month working at the huge expanse of ocean called the Great Barrier Reef, return to Japan for five days or so, and then leave immediately for Siberia for nine weeks. For around three months I wouldn't be able to be with Gaku, either as his father or his friend.

I told Gaku that night, after he had been fishing for Gaku from our second-story veranda. He looked thoughtful for a while, then said, "Oh."

Scratching his crew-cut head with both hands, he added with an atypical pout, "You would have to go at the best time of year. That's when we could go bottom fishing or even fish for some striped beakperch."

"Come to think of it," I said, "I guess I wasn't around much in November last year either, was I?" I knew I shouldn't have mentioned it, but it was too late.

"That's right. You went to the South Pole."

"No, I didn't make it that time. We had to turn back

on the way."

"See? You screw up everything, Pa."

"Hey, at least I tried."

Gaku turned aside and said, "I really wish we could go ocean fishing again. You know, somewhere like Miyake Island."

Our earlier expedition to catch amberjack off Miyake had been a truly enjoyable vacation for me, but we had come home empty-handed. I went to my room and checked my calendar. I was scheduled to leave in only ten days, and an overnight fishing trip to the coast hardly seemed possible, but there was one Sunday free. I went back to Gaku's room and asked him, "You want to go fishing for mudsuckers?"

His usual happy-boy face returned in a flash. "We can go anywhere as long as it's by the sea," he said.

I called Noda that same day, and the instant I mentioned mudsuckers he said, "That's a great idea." Noda was the type who never complained about his workload or his schedule being this or that. He probably always had tons of writing to do himself, but I never once heard him say so. To Noda, the most important thing in life was to have fun. I have never mentioned this to Noda, but sometimes he seems exactly like Gaku.

Sunday was hardly a nice fall day for mudsucker fishing; it was cold, with intermittent showers. We met Noda as agreed at a station near Tokyo Disneyland, so despite the weather and the fact that it was morning, the station was already jammed with families. Closer inspection also showed that several other people were apparently going fishing. When Gaku noticed this he grew impatient.

"Come on," he urged irritably in front of a store that I had entered to buy bait. "Let's hurry!"

"Don't worry," I said. "There's at least fifty thousand mudsuckers out there this time of year."

Noda added, "Yeah, and when I looked at the river from the

train on the way here, there were about fifty thousand people fishing for them, too."

Gaku made a face, as if to say, "See? I told you!"

When we arrived at the expanse of river we had chosen, we saw that it was true. The river was already swarming with people. There were people with rods fishing from the banks, and there were people fishing off boats, their nylon jacket collars upturned against a chilly wind.

We made our way to a boat rental shop, but the old man running the place shook his head, as if to tell us we were naive to assume there would be any boats left.

"Do you think," I asked, "it will be very long before any boats are returned?"

"Well, let's see now," replied a ruddy-faced matron who was apparently his wife. "A bit after noon, say around two o'clock, folks with kids start coming back. The little ones get sick of fishing, see?" Then she pointed to a raft made of oil drums right next to a landing pier. "If you folks want to," she said, "I reckon you can wait over there."

It was a strange-looking raft, and it had a telephone booth-sized, galvanized-iron structure perched in the middle of it.

"What's that?" I asked.

"It's a toilet for them that are out fishing in boats," the woman said, her face brightening in the chill wind. "But it's real clean, 'cause we don't let it back up."

We climbed on the toilet raft to discover it was a pretty good place to fish from. It was about three meters by two meters, and the toilet was perched in the middle of it. Opening the door revealed a square hole, through which everything was apparently discharged into the river.

"Hey, Gaku," Noda said, "you could do some hole fishing here, and it'd be just like sniggling for pond smelt."

"Wow, no kidding, that's great!" my boy said. He seemed

seriously to believe it would be a good idea.

We put down our bags, staked out our fishing positions, and started tying our lines. Noda pulled out a bottle of bourbon. "When the wind's this nippy," he said, "this stuff comes in handy."

Noda and I were taking sips and still leisurely tying our lines when Gaku suddenly announced, "Here they come!" and pulled in the first fish. He had been constantly rehearsing for this moment ever since we had decided to go fishing for mudsuckers, and sure enough, despite the fact that it was his first time, he worked fast.

"This is fun," he commented. "It's just like they said in the book. You can feel 'em bite the way the rod shakes."

"Attaboy, Gaku," Noda said, taking a slug of whiskey from an aluminum cup. "Keep it up and we'll have tempura tonight."

"Pa, you and Mr. Noda better hurry," Gaku said. "There's fifty thousand other people here, you know."

"Aah," I answered, "but true pros always start off slowly, at their own pace."

Then Gaku yelled, "I got another one! And it's even bigger than the first!"

I didn't catch as many fish as I thought I would. Maybe it was because I spent too much time drinking whiskey with Noda and therefore didn't concentrate properly on the tip of my rod, but after two hours Gaku had pulled in fourteen fish, whereas Noda and I together had only caught five.

Eventually there was nothing left in the round whiskey bottle.

After a word with the old man running the boat rental operation, I climbed off the raft and went to a local store to buy something more to drink and eat. I bought whiskey, beer, and some snacks, and by the time I got back to the toilet raft Noda was already boiling water on his Radius stove and cooking

123

instant noodles. Around the same time—earlier than I had expected—one of the rowboats became available and was assigned to us.

As we ate our noodles, I told Noda about my upcoming trip. Since I wouldn't be around at New Year's, I asked him if it would be all right for Gaku to spend some time with him at Lake Kameyama during his winter vacation.

It turned out that the two of them had already decided the matter between themselves. As soon as Gaku's holidays began, he and his fishing buddies from school, To-chan and Mi-chan, were going to take their tent to Noda's place.

"It'll really be an interesting New Year when those kids arrive," said Noda with a laugh.

Feeling inexplicably happy, I pulled the pop-top off a can of beer with an exaggerated gesture and a pwoosh. "Just think, Gaku," I said. "You can go kayaking and fishing every day this winter vacation."

Gaku looked at us as if he were the head of a family rather than the child. "Yeah," he said, "but you and Mr. Noda had better get serious about fishing instead of just sitting there drinking. Otherwise we won't have mudsucker tempura tonight."

I resolved to fish a little more seriously, as Gaku put it, and make our tempura dinner come true. Gaku and I decided to climb in the rowboat and go in search of a better fishing spot. We tied a creel we'd bought at the tackle shop in front of the station to the side of the boat, stowed a bag of tangerines aboard, and cast off.

The creel already held the seventeen or so fish that Gaku had caught, so I told him that if we could just match the number, we would probably have enough for our tempura dinner plan.

We began rowing, and discovered that most of the other boats on the river were concentrated near the banks: the middle of the river was fairly empty. It somehow seemed as though we would be able to catch more fish near the farthest bank, so I plied the oars to direct us there. But after we reached our destination and tossed out our lines, we soon realized that there would be no dramatic change in our luck and that neither we nor the other boats near us were going to have any more success than we had from the toilet raft. Gaku caught two fish, but I didn't even get a nibble.

Other people parked under a nearby bridge seemed to be raising and lowering their rods fairly often. "Well, Gaku," I said, "it seems as though this place isn't that great, after all. Maybe we should try our luck under the bridge over there."

We moved to the bridge, but it wasn't much different.

"Well," I said, "I guess this place is not so good either."

"Maybe it's better by the toilet raft, after all," Gaku said.

There were lots of shallows and exposed pilings under the bridge. I had just decided to detour around the shallows and head for the toilet raft when disaster struck.

Gaku suddenly yelled, "Oh, no! What happened?" sounding as if he were about to burst into tears. I looked where he was pointing, and saw our creel; to my astonishment, a big rip had appeared in part of the netting, and most of the goby inside had escaped.

"And after I caught all those fish!" Gaku moaned. As he always did when terribly upset, he looked down and jammed his clenched fist in the middle of his face.

I pulled up our creel in a panic, but there were only seven very dead goby left inside; the live ones had all fled. I didn't know when the netting had been torn, but I suddenly realized I must have been fairly intoxicated when it occurred. I had drunk more than I'd meant to, and while engaging in some power rowing in my inebriated state, the creel must have caught on one of the pilings.

I looked around and noticed it was already getting dark. The wind had suddenly turned much colder. Catching that many fish again was out of the question. I did the only thing I could think of: I apologized.

"I'm sorry, Gaku," I said. "Your pa was careless. Forgive, me, okay?"

Gaku looked me straight in the eye and said with a worried look, "You sure it's all right if we can't make tempura?"

With the five mudsuckers that Noda and I had caught off the toilet raft earlier we only had a total of twelve fish, but we decided to take them home and ask my wife to make tempura with them after all. Noda had to come get his dog, so he was going to spend the night at our place anyway.

As compensation for the loss of Gaku's goby, I agreed to treat him, as usual, to noodles and fried dumplings.

"But you know what, Pa?" Gaku said with a serious expression. "This time you've gotta give me half as much noodles again for every day you're late with your 'combenzation.' I've gotta do that 'cause you're always so slow in carrying out your promises. This way, the later you are, the more noodles I'll get to eat, so it's a good deal for me, too."

"Understood," I said. "It can be noodles from any restaurant, right?"

"Yeah. But I like the ones at Daishoken best."

"Understood," I said again.

Back home, my wife served up a big tempura dish of our twelve fish with assorted vegetables and fried clams. I restrained myself, and only ate two of the smallest ones.

We let Gaku the dog inside again because Dai wouldn't give him a minute's peace. Little Gaku licked big Gaku's feet and mournfully howled, "Aroof-Aroof."

NINE

The Two-Day Present

I returned from Australia and New Guinea at the end of November. As usual when coming back from overseas, I got in a taxi at Narita airport and headed straight down the highway. It normally took around two hours to travel through Tokyo to my home outside the city, but after being away so long I always enjoyed seeing the familiar sights slip by outside the car window.

I felt the late fall scenery of Japan gently seep into my soul. For the last month I had been traveling between Australia and New Guinea, mostly scuba diving, working my way north toward the equator along the nearly two-thousand-kilometer-long Great Barrier Reef. All my days and nights had been spent in the Southern hemisphere, where it was midsummer. Only two days earlier I had been living with grass-skirted natives on a tiny island in New Guinea called Kitava, eating taro roots and yams for supper under the light of a gas lantern.

As I gazed at the passing Tokyo landscape, I reflected on the fact that since my flight had arrived early in the morning, I would reach my house around eleven. My wife had taken the day off and would be at home, but since it was a weekday Gaku would still be at school. Part of me approved of this, and part of me felt a vague sense of letdown.

In the past, I had usually returned from long overseas trips at night. Gaku would often still be up, waiting for me at the risk of angering his mother, and as soon as he heard the thud of my heavy suitcase in the hallway, he would dash out of his bedroom and cling to me. This had lasted until around third grade and then it had stopped, perhaps because he became more self-conscious. Instead, he began to grab me like the professional wrestlers we always imitated, and butt his shaved head into my midriff. He probably just hoped that I had brought him a present, but he always seemed so genuinely happy to see me that it warmed my heart.

Three months before, when I had returned from a trip to Sri Lanka, his reaction had been a bit different. I had arrived home around ten at night, and he had just stared at me with his hands stuck in the pockets of his sweat pants and grinned. Then he had said, "You're back, huh?" The days of butting his head into me were clearly over.

While eating a late dinner with my wife that night, I had remarked, "Gaku's really growing up, isn't he? Whenever I come back from these long trips I can tell how much he's changing year by year just by the way he greets me."

"Oh, really?" she said, with a surprised look.

"Sure, when he was little he used to dash out to hug me as soon as I reached the door."

"Why, come to think of it, you're right. He doesn't do that any more, does he?"

"No, he doesn't. "Course, he's a lot bigger now, so if he did I'd be in trouble."

"Yes, and it would look pretty weird, too," my wife had said.

This time I was returning before noon on a weekday, so Gaku was at school and I wouldn't get to see his latest way of welcoming me. I had a confused feeling that this was both good and bad.

The taxi left the Central Expressway and entered Koshu Avenue. I noticed that the leaves of the ginkgo trees lining the road had turned completely yellow, and that many were already scattered over the ground below. I saw a young man riding his bicycle beside the row of trees and wearing a scarf, and it seemed strange: only two days ago, I recalled, my companions and I had been besieged by curious New Guineans wearing nothing but grass skirts. In just a month, Tokyo had turned quite cold.

When I reached home my wife was waiting for me with breakfast ready. She looked at me, rolled her eyes, and said, "You're even more tanned than you were last summer."

"I can't help it," I replied. "It was beautiful weather every day, and the sun was blazing hot."

"And now you're off to a place that's just the opposite, right?"

"Uh-huh. That's what they tell me, at least."

I had not had hot rice and miso soup for a long time, and it tasted wonderful. It felt warm and comfortable being home, but I knew I would only be able to enjoy the sensation for another week. On December sixth I had to leave for Siberia. I was going to be gone for over two months and would not return until the following February.

One of the main purposes of my trip was to visit one of the coldest spots in the Northern hemisphere—Oymyakon, in eastern Siberia, where according to advance reports the temperature would be around minus seventy degrees centigrade in mid-

December. Having just returned from a land where summer was in full swing, I only had one week to condition myself physically before going to a land of extreme cold. And since I had been away for one month and was about to be away again for two, I had a ton of work to do in the interim. The trip to Siberia was virtually an expedition, and it would require an enormous amount of preparation: meeting the other members of my party, testing equipment to make sure it could withstand the cold, and packing. On top of that, I also had to write pieces for two magazines in which my work was being serialized. Just thinking about it all was depressing.

I sipped some piping hot green tea and grumbled to myself: "And I only have one week...."

"Gaku's worried," my wife suddenly announced.

"About what?" I asked.

"Well, you were gone all of December last year, too, remember? When he learned you were going to be gone from December to February this year, he started worrying that he might not get any Christmas or New Year's presents. He was upset last year because you skipped his Christmas present, you know."

"So that's what he's worried about!" I had assumed he was concerned for my personal safety on the trip, and I had been pleasantly surprised by his apparent thoughtfulness. But it hadn't been that at all. Around the same time a year ago, I recalled, I had been traveling over a glacier in Patagonia, near the South Pole. I had returned at year-end and given Gaku a New Year's present of a sleeping bag and a rod with a reel, but I had missed Christmas. And that was the last time he had butted his still-shaved head into my chest.

"Now I get it," I said, staring at the calendar on the kitchen wall. "This is the second year in a row, isn't it?"

I knew I was going to be murderously busy in the one week I had left, but then and there I resolved to devote myself to Gaku for two whole days. It just so happened that there was a weekend coming up, so I decided I would use that Saturday and Sunday to indulge his consuming passion—I would take him on a fishing trip. We would have one night and two days. We would go to a hot spring inn someplace on the coast, and I would present him with the chance to do some saltwater fishing. It might also be a chance to give my weary body some rest.

When Gaku came home from school, he spotted me and commented, "Oh, you're back!" Then, with a slight variation on the expression he had greeted me with when I had returned from Sri Lanka, he announced: "I'm starved!"

Some time ago the boy had unilaterally decided that he had to have four square meals a day, so whenever he returned from school he usually stuffed himself with some instant noodles or thin somen noodles that he fixed himself. The previous summer, when he had first told me that he was making himself some chilled Chinese noodles, I had asked him how, and he had told me that he boiled instant noodles, rinsed them in cold water, and then added his own special sauce. When I had asked him where he learned how to make the sauce, he had stated, as serious as could be, that he had found a simple recipe for it in a book titled *Chinese Noodles*, and, moreover, that the secret was to use sesame oil. To my amazement, it turned out that he had been studying the cookbooks on our kitchen shelf by himself and following the recipes in them. That was when I realized that—in the way he was so bound and determined to eat what he wanted and do what he wanted—my son bore an uncanny resemblance to me, and to the way I led my life.

As Gaku prepared some noodles before my eyes with incredible speed, he gave me a sidelong glance and said with a frown, "By the way, I know you're going off on a trip again, but, like I told Ma, I hope you don't forget about my Christmas and New Year's presents this year."

"Don't worry," I said. Then, making a deliberate attempt to impress him, I added, "What if we make one of the presents a little saltwater fishing trip?"

"It's a deal!" he immediately replied, adding, "Think we could go to Miyake?"

The two of us had gone fishing on Miyake Island the previous summer. Ever since, he had been telling me how much he wanted to go again.

"I don't think we can make Miyake this time," I answered, "because I don't think I can get plane tickets on such short notice. I was thinking maybe we could go somewhere like the Izu Peninsula instead."

He thought for a minute and said, "You mean around Ito, where we went before, right? Yeah, I guess that'd be okay, but I'd really like to go someplace where we could do both surf and breakwater fishing."

I checked the maps and train schedules and learned that Inatori would probably be the easiest place to go in Izu. Wherever we went, we would have to leave home early Saturday morning or we wouldn't have much time to fish at all. I discussed the matter with my wife, and we decided to let Gaku play hooky from his Saturday classes at school. I told him this and he nodded, laughed, and said, "That's a great idea."

I quickly reserved a room at an inn in Inatori, and then set about scheduling my own work. My remaining six days would be horribly hectic, but I was determined that nothing would interfere with my plans for Saturday and Sunday. I might have to stay up all night, but I would record three months' worth of programs for the FM radio station where I had been working for two years, as well as the narration for a TV documentary shot when I was diving in Australia. I somehow managed to keep the weekend open. I knew that if anything changed and I had to break my promise to Gaku, I would be miserable during my entire two months in Siberia.

On Friday night, from the lobby of the FM radio station in Tokyo's Shinjuku district, I phoned home and asked for Gaku. He came on the line, and in the voice that always seemed deep for a young boy, said, "That you, Pa?"

"Yes. Listen, Gaku, you have to get up at five A.M. tomorrow or we won't make it. Get your fishing gear ready and hit the sack early tonight, okay?"

"I'm all ready to go, Pa. I read in a book that opaleye and marbled rockfish are biting at Izu in December, so I packed stuff for that."

"Well, don't forget to pack the clothes you need, too. It's probably cold, and you'd better take some rain gear, too."

"I know, I know. I packed some tackle for you, too." His voice was awfully excited, but that was no wonder considering he was going to skip school and go saltwater fishing the next day.

I continued my recording work for the FM station until one in the morning, and then decided to go home and come back to finish the rest late Monday night. I got in a taxi, told the driver the general direction I wanted to go, laid down on the back seat, and immediately fell asleep.

The next morning, sure enough, Gaku woke up at five o'clock sharp. Normally he never stirred when I called him, but this time, as always when we went fishing, it took only a couple of words and he was up in a flash. I, on the other hand, had only had around three hours of sleep in bed. I was bone-tired and frankly would have preferred to continue slumbering away.

My wife came up the stairs with the just-delivered morning paper and said, "The weather report says it's going to get worse from today, so be sure to pack your rain gear."

I checked Gaku's rucksack to make sure he had his raincoat, and then in mine I tossed an incredibly tough field parka for longshoremen that I had bought in Brisbane, Australia.

Our train—"Odoriko No. 1"—was scheduled to leave Tokyo station at eight A.M., and when we arrived at the station platform we were pleasantly surprised to find the cars nearly deserted. We hadn't eaten anything for breakfast, so we bought box lunches—one pork and one special Western-style—and tea. Then we boarded, placed our purchases on the windowsill beside our seats, turned to each other, and grinned.

"Well, young man," I said teasingly, "aren't you supposed to be in school today?"

Gaku said nothing, but he crooked his arm and began elbowing me in the ribs.

"Okay! Okay!" I protested, cracking up. "I won't tell anyone that Gaku Shiina's playing hooky so he can go fishing!"

He merely jabbed me in the ribs even harder.

Our train started rolling, and we began eating our box lunches. Until around Shinagawa Station we were running at the same speed as another train on the Keihin-Tohoku line, and when Gaku saw its cars, jam-packed with morning commuters, he said, "I bet they're all looking at us and feeling jealous." Then he stuffed his mouth with a huge amount of rice, made a little-boy face, and laughed: "Heh heh heh."

We finished our box lunches and Gaku began reading a book on fishing. I opened a book about Siberia, but not long after I fell asleep. When I next opened my eyes the train was already running along the coast and Gaku was shaking me hard, trying to wake me up.

"Pa!" he said, looking alternately at my face and the ocean outside. "They just announced we'll be at Inatori in three or four stops!"

"We will?" I said. "All right!" I didn't know what I really meant by "All right!" but after having slept like a log for nearly two hours, I finally felt rested.

"The ocean looks pretty calm," Gaku said, staring at the sea the whole time. "I can see some people fishing."

The weather forecast had apparently been accurate. Both the sea and the sky above it looked dark and heavy.

We hailed a taxi in front of Inatori Station and went straight to the inn where I had reservations. The front desk clerk, who had a slight stoop, said with a mildly disgusted look, "Listen, your room isn't quite ready yet. After all, the party that stayed in it last night just checked out. I won't be able to let you in the room until around three o'clock." He seemed to be saying that coming so early to a hot spring inn betrayed a lack of common sense.

"Oh, that's all right," I said. "We came to do some fishing, so if we could just store our bags someplace until this evening, that'd be fine."

The stooped clerk finally smiled in a businesslike fashion, and with a mincing nod pointed to a space behind the front desk. "Well, in that case," he said, "we'll keep your luggage for you here."

Gaku had brought along a fairly detailed map titled *The Best Fishing Spots in the Kanto Region*, so we consulted it and learned that a breakwater near a red lighthouse was the best spot in the area to catch opaleye. We had the inn call a taxi for us, and we asked the driver to take us to a tackle shop near the lighthouse.

A woman in her fifties was minding the shop when we arrived. I knew Gaku probably hadn't brought along all the equipment we would need, so I said, "We're here to fish for some opaleye, and we'd, er, like to buy the right bait and hooks."

I had never seriously fished until Gaku became obsessed with the sport, so in reality I knew almost none of the correct terminology, or, for that matter, even how to fish. Frankly, I didn't even know how to tie a leader to a main line. Gaku (who had no interest in anything except comic books, noodles, and fishing) went fishing in the local rivers and ponds whenever he had a free moment, and read books on fishing and studied how to tie lines and how to fish. To me—his father—his level of knowledge was downright astounding. But I knew that wasn't the way it looked to people in bait and tackle shops. To them, I was a typical father fishing on his days off, with his son in tow.

The moment I mentioned fishing for opaleye, the woman launched into an explanation that I only half understood. I heard everything, but the fishing terms eluded me. Gaku appeared to comprehend, however, for he said in a tiny voice, "I've got some of those, but our fish hooks seem a little too big."

An interesting thing about Gaku was that—although he was a fifth grader strong enough to beat up sixth graders, and was rapidly turning into a "young man" with enough character to ignore his mother at home—he still shrank and spoke shyly in front of adults he did not know. It always seemed so out of character that when he did this I nearly burst out laughing, and it always started with his voice suddenly becoming very soft. I assumed this was due to normal young-boy shyness, but I also knew it was something I could rib him about later if the need arose.

"You've got to speak louder, Gaku," I said, pretending to be irritated. "And make sure you buy now whatever we're going to need."

"I know, I know," he said, looking at me with something like a glare, "but we really oughta learn a little more about this area before we buy anything."

The woman manning the store looked back and forth between Gaku and me, apparently thinking we were quite an unusual father and son. "Well, what'll you have for bait?" she said. "Around here lots of folks scatter groundbait and use some small krill."

"Do you have any No. 7 eyeless live bait hooks?" Gaku

asked in a tiny, bashful voice.

"We do, but you have to tie a leader on the No. 7. You sure you folks can do it yourselves?" The woman spoke in a confused sort of way, as if she weren't sure whether she should be addressing me or Gaku.

"We can do it," Gaku said, rather curtly.

Attaboy, Gaku. Way-to-go, I thought. He had replied with a surprising directness, and, overly proud father that I am, I secretly applauded him. I myself had tried tying an eyeless hook on a leader once before, but it had required such incredible concentration and dexterity that I had given up.

"I see," the woman said. "Well, in that case you're right, it would be best to use a No. 7." She had clearly begun to direct her speech and fix her attention on Gaku.

"How deep should we run our lines?" Gaku asked.

"Well, let's see," she said, "if you're using a No. 7, then one fathom ought to do."

"Gotcha," Gaku said. The dialogue had become one between experts.

"Anything biting out there besides opaleye?" I asked. On a previous occasion, with Gaku as my teacher, I had caught a little amberjack and it had been an unforgettably pleasant experience. It had required heaving my line way out into the ocean, and if possible I wanted to try that again.

"Do you think, for example," I continued, "that we could catch anything in the lighthouse area with bottom fishing?" I was certain that that was the simple, almost crude, style of fishing that I had used to catch the amberjack off Miyake.

Gaku suddenly crooked his elbow, jabbed me in the ribs, and glared at me. Ignoring what I had just said, he asked the woman, "Do you have any musselworms?"

"Why, sure," she replied, "but they're pretty expensive now."

"Okay, well in that case I'll just take one package," he said.

"Oh, and we'll also need a few swivels." He spoke more softly than he normally did with me, but his voice was clear and firm.

I thought about the time when, to compensate for my trip to Australia, we had gone fishing for mudsuckers near Disneyland, and how I had accidentally torn our creel and lost over half the fish Gaku had caught. We were trying to travel light this time, and we hadn't even brought an ice chest with us.

"Say, Gaku," I said, "don't we need a creel?"

He looked up at me and shook his head with the same disapproving expression he had used earlier.

"What are we going to do if we catch some fish?" I asked. "We've got to have one, right?" The last time we had bought a cheap creel, so this time I was prepared to buy one that was tough and well made, even if it was expensive.

"We need one, right?" I repeated seriously, a little surprised at his reaction.

"No!" he answered, glaring at me again. "We don't need a creel!"

Try as I might, I couldn't understand why we didn't need one.

We started to leave the store, and I realized that although it was still not yet noon the sky had grown considerably darker. The woman waiting on us saw us to the door, and in a kindly voice said, "Too bad it looks like rain this afternoon. Actually, though, the fish bite better on days like this."

The breakwater by the lighthouse was fairly high above the surface of the sea. Four men in their fifties stood on the end of it silently holding their fishing rods out in front of them, looking as though they lived to fish.

When we reached the edge of the breakwater, there were hardly any waves, but the wind was quite chilly. The surface of the ocean had turned dark and if one squinted at the horizon one could barely tell where the sea met the thickening layer of clouds above it.

We put our things down on the ground below the lighthouse and quickly pulled out our fishing gear. I knew nothing about fishing for opaleye, or even what kind of tackle to use, so Gaku had to tie the tiny hooks on the leaders and attach the floats and some weights called "split shots." Since I was good for little else, I concentrated on putting the reels on the rods and divvying up the block of dried possum shrimp groundbait.

As usual, Gaku first tied a leader to my rod, and then busied himself with his own. For some reason, I felt terribly embarrassed by this. I couldn't help thinking that to people with a conventional view of parents and children, our roles would seem topsy-turvy.

"Okay, Pa, here we go," Gaku said, crouching below the lighthouse with his fanny windward, and returning to his normal tone of voice. "Remember, the tails of these krill we're using for bait are the toughest part, so the first thing you've gotta do is run the hook through 'em like this, see? If you don't do it right, they fall off right away."

"Gotcha," I said. In the past, whenever I had fished without getting a nibble, that was exactly the first thing I had always worried about—whether there was any bait left on the hook at the end of my line. Usually I became impatient and reeled in, and then Gaku got angry at me. If our bait was easy to lose, I was going to be very, very careful this time.

The fishermen around us seemed like true regulars, but close inspection showed that their rods were not moving up and down very vigorously. I heard the creaking sound of someone reeling in, and I turned around to look. One man had managed to catch a tiny bluespotted boxfish, but that was all.

Neither Gaku's rod nor mine performed very satisfactorily, either. I apparently was not attaching my bait properly after all, because when I reeled in my line after fishing a bit the krill bait was usually gone. After an hour or so Gaku hooked a little wrasse and I caught a bluespotted boxfish. And then it finally started to drizzle, slowly and steadily building up into full-fledged rain. Soon Gaku and I and the four other anglers presented a pathetic picture, huddled in our raincoats.

When it was past two in the afternoon I proposed to Gaku that we go eat lunch somewhere and get out of the rain. Frankly, I was sick of fishing in the rain without any success. But my boy—who normally declared he had to eat four times a day—was willing to ignore his empty stomach and forgo a bowl of noodles for the thrill of staring at the tip of his fishing rod. He nodded to acknowledge my suggestion and said, "Seems like something's tugging on my line every once in a while, so let's hang in there another thirty minutes or so."

I haggled desperately with him over the thirty minutes, and knocked it down to fifteen, but by the time we finally packed up our fishing gear it was nearly three o'clock. Two of the fishermen near us were getting ready to leave.

On the path back from the breakwater, sprays of rain blew up at us from foot level, carried by gusts of wind from the sea. While dodging them I yelled to Gaku, "Guess we didn't have any luck today. Too bad about all this rain, but at least we have the whole day tomorrow to try again."

Turning his head like me to avoid the rain and wind, he said, "Yeah, but actually the fish don't care about the rain at all. It said so in a book I read. You oughta know that from your scuba diving, Pa."

"Yeah, I guess you're right."

Although I had just returned from my diving trip, the blue sea and blue sky of Australia and New Guinea already seemed like a distant memory. But as we tramped through the rain I thought how much I would someday like to show my son the wonderful undersea world I had experienced. Once, when twenty meters under the sea near the Great Barrier Reef, I had looked up at the surface and seen several hundred varieties of big and little fish. One three-meter-long giant—a member of the sea bass family called a "giant potato cod"—even came and stared at me from thirty centimeters away, making absolutely no attempt to flee. It was I who had felt like fleeing.

We decided to eat lunch at a noodle shop we found near the train station. Since it was already three o'clock and we would soon check into the inn and be served a variety of seafood dishes, I proposed to Gaku that we eat lightly, and he casually agreed. The eatery was called Fukutei, and at night it apparently transformed into a pub, for the shelves behind the counter were lined with dozens of whiskey bottles kept for individual regular customers.

We entered and found a fiftyish old timer minding the shop, reading a sports newspaper with his chin propped on his hands. He looked up at us with quadruple bags under his eyes and said in an astonishingly high-pitched voice, "Too bad about the weather." Then he folded his paper and added, "Catch anything?"

"Nope, not a thing," I confessed.

"Really? That's a shame," he said. "Yesterday people were pulling in foot-long opaleye."

"It's okay," I answered. "We're here just to have fun, anyway."

We stacked our fishing tackle next to the entrance, took off our rain gear, sat down, and realized we were famished.

"Well," I asked Gaku, "what'll it be?"

"I'd like some noodles and fried dumplings," he said. Then, apparently remembering what I had told him earlier about saving room for the sashimi and other seafood dishes we were sure to be served later at the inn, he added with an unusually discerning look, "But I suppose I shouldn't, huh?"

"Well," I replied, "that's true. Why don't we order one bowl of noodles and one plate of dumplings and share them?"

"Okay," he said. "That's fine with me."

The sound of the rain falling on the eaves of the shop's tin roof seemed to be growing in strength and intensity.

The rain continued through the night. At the inn, we were given a room on the seventh floor with a view of the sea, and that evening we faced each other over a low table in our room and ate an embarrassingly deluxe dinner. I say "embarrassingly" because the woman who served us did so in such an extravagant fashion, even roasting abalone on an alcohol burner on the table right in front of us. The abalone was still alive, and it trembled, shuddered, and emitted a white froth as if suffering terribly.

The woman said this particular dish was called "dancing abalone," and that it was a specialty of the inn. As soon as the flame was out—she told us over and over again—we should dip it in soy sauce and eat it. Then she left the room.

After the woman disappeared, Gaku said almost apologetically, "I don't know why, but I sort of feel sorry for the abalone."

"I know. I feel the same way," I responded. I couldn't think of anything else to say.

Gaku plowed into a bowl of rice and his favorite side order of sashimi. Then he wolfed down a steamed egg-custard and asked, "Can I watch TV now?"

I took a drink of beer. This was the first opportunity I had had in a month to sit down and really talk with my own son, and here he was, only interested in a new TV series due to start that night.

While listening to the sound of the TV show, I finished my beer, and then I drank the whiskey I had in a pocket flask. After unwinding earlier with Gaku in the inn's hot spring bath, the alcohol seemed to course through my veins far faster than usual.

Outside, the rain continued to fall. Before retiring for the night, Gaku and I decided to do some early morning fishing on a little breakwater in front of the inn.

I woke the next morning at the six-thirty wakeup call. It was late fall in Izu Peninsula and it was still dark outside, but true to form, as soon as Gaku heard me say the word fishing, his body twitched and his eyes popped open. Then he stood up jerkily and made his way to the bathroom, crashing into the wall and the paper sliding doors of the room. I decided that his physical body was still mostly asleep, and that the words going fishing had probably acted as a magic incantation, enabling him to wake up on willpower alone.

When Gaku returned from the bathroom, he was still half-asleep, so I opened the windows and let cold morning air fill every corner of the room. "Hurry up, wash your face and get dressed," I ordered.

He made no reply, but he plopped down on top of his futon and began to strip off his pajamas energetically, shivering and muttering about the cold.

The rain had completely stopped during the night, and it looked, with luck, as though the morning sun might come up. I stared at the dark, predawn surface of the ocean and could make out a few wave caps breaking near the shore. Outside our window the wind occasionally gusted past with a piercing groan, but since it rarely entered our room, I knew it was blowing toward the ocean that day. Just when I was wondering what effect such a strong wind from the land would have on the fishing, I heard Gaku's husky voice behind me: "Hurry up, Pa. Let's go."

The stooped clerk from the day before was still manning the front desk with tired-looking eyes. He produced a facsimile of a smile, commented on how early we were, and in a bad attempt at a joke advised us to "bring something good home for breakfast."

The breakwater in front of the inn was very small and had

many tetrapods piled up on the sea side of it, so it didn't seem like a very good spot to fish. Huge swells surged toward the pilings, and even more powerful blasts of wind from the land swept over their crests, scattering the white spray that shot up as the waves hit the breakwater. Because the wind was so strong it was much colder on the breakwater than I had anticipated.

Gaku handed me a casting rod he had already rigged for me and said, "At times like this it's best to use floats, but I hope we'll be able to see 'em move."

The wind was blowing from behind us, so it would be easy to cast our lines out, but if we cast them too far into the heavy swells it would be hard to spot the floats when the fish took the bait.

While rigging his own rod and looking back and forth between me and the ocean, Gaku said, "I think we'd better draw ourselves in tight until it gets a little lighter."

"What do you mean 'draw ourselves in tight'?" I asked.

Clearly disgusted by my question, he said in a loud voice, "Just crank your reel . . . you know, just turn the handle toward you!"

I thought about it and realized it was the only logical thing to do. After casting, I cranked my reel at high speed, and in the faintly growing light I saw my float rapidly drawing nearer, pertly dancing between the wave troughs.

Dawn was fast approaching. A promontory of land way around the other side of the bay—which only an instant before had been impossible to make out—now floated dimly purple on the horizon. And looking in the direction the wind was blowing, I could see an expanding band of clouds. They were catching the light of the rising sun and beginning to glow orange red.

People in other rooms at the inn had a clear view of us fishing out on the edge of the breakwater, and, sure enough, before long we were joined by a couple of groups of men with hung-over looks, wearing quilted kimonos and clacking the heels of their geta clogs on the ground as they walked.

They apparently thought I was a typical fishing father who had coerced his poor son into coming along with him, for they went up to Gaku and began offering advice he didn't really need, telling him he should cast his rod more directly in front of him, or that he hadn't attached his musselworms properly. But one thing about Gaku is that the only grown man he really trusts is Tomosuke Noda; he was discouragingly unresponsive. The men, for their part, had just emerged from the hot spring baths in the inn and had nonchalantly walked out in their robes to have a look at us. As soon as they realized how ferocious the wind was out on the end of the breakwater, however, and as soon as they knew they would be unable to stand more than five minutes of it, they promptly turned around and went back inside.

Gaku eventually caught a fish shaped like a red snapper, which I couldn't identify. I had to have him show me how to do everything, and merely stood there brandishing my rod in the wind like a rank amateur. I didn't hook a thing.

We returned to the inn to find breakfast ready for us. It was your very average Japanese inn breakfast, consisting of dried fillet of mackerel, seaweed, and raw egg, but after our early morning efforts it tasted rather good; we ate silently, and each of us had three bowls of rice. This particular inn seemed to have a deliberate policy of getting the guests to leave as soon as possible after breakfast, for right after our maid finished clearing off the table in our room she brought us the bill and began asking us over and over, "All packed and ready to go?" and "Shall I call a cab for you now?"

We had a return reservation on the express leaving Inatori Station at 3:26 P.M., so in fact we had plenty of time. Before heading for the station, therefore, we took a taxi to the lighthouse again. Unlike the day before, the sky was beautifully clear, but huge swells were smashing into the rock wall and incredibly powerful winds were gusting every which way. Perhaps because of this, although we had expected a crowd of anglers, there was not a soul in sight. We walked out to the edge of the breakwater to see if we could fish and were nearly blown off by the gusts, so we knew that it was out of the question. Over on a road a ways off from the breakwater we could see cardboard boxes and crumpled newspapers tumbling over and over through the air.

"No fishing here today, Gaku," I said. "Let's find someplace without so much wind." He had been all fired up to try his hand under the lighthouse again and hook a whopper of an opaleye, so when I said this he looked terribly crestfallen.

We started walking toward the inside of the harbor and caught sight of a lone man fishing beneath a breakwater where there was a little white beacon light. It was in an area sheltered by the lighthouse, with fewer crashing swells, and it seemed safe.

"Okay," I said, "let's bag ourselves a few opaleye over there."

As soon as I said this, Gaku—who until that point had looked miserable and been grimly silent—sternly announced, "Listen, Pa, there's one thing about fishing you should know. You can't always expect to catch the same type of fish everywhere. The only place opaleye bite near here is around that lighthouse and that place called Kasagoppala where they have those big boulders." Then, pointing toward the breakwater area by the beacon light, he said, "If we go over there with the lines we've got rigged now we won't be able to catch anything!"

"And by the way," he continued, scowling at me, "yesterday at the tackle shop you said you wanted to try bottom fishing. But you know what? Stuff like that really embarrasses me. Ninety-nine percent of the anglers don't do bottom fishing around the breakwaters this time of year. The old lady in the tackle shop must have been laughing at you!"

Come to think of it, Gaku had elbowed me in the ribs when I mentioned bottom fishing in the store. At the time I had just wondered why he was doing it and hadn't understood what he meant.

The breakwater with the beacon light was divided into two levels. We walked along the upper level, and the wind was still blowing hard. The solitary angler we had spotted earlier was sitting on the lower level out of the wind, nonchalantly smoking a cigarette. Gaku ran over to him to ask something, and then came back and said, "He said he's fishing for sand smelt. See? Just like I told you, you have to go after different fish in different places. And I didn't bring anything to catch sand smelt with."

I knew that Gaku had been looking forward to catching some opaleye by the lighthouse, and that he was now in a sulk. But there wasn't anything I could do about it. At a loss for words, I remained silent.

"What the heck," he said, "we'll just have to fish for sand smelt after all. Give me a thousand yen, Pa. I'll go back to that bait shop where the old lady was yesterday and buy some stuff."

I fished a thousand-yen note out of my wallet and said, "You be careful, okay? The wind's awfully strong, and I don't want you to be blown into the ocean."

Gaku scowled as if to say, Man, it's stuff like this that really bugs me, and announced, "Listen, Pa. I'm a person. I'm not a cat or a cardboard box, and a little wind like this isn't going to blow me away." Then he crammed the fist with the thousand-yen note into his pocket, and with the wind roaring around his head and his body leaning forward at an angle, he strode off toward the tackle shop on the road by the sea.

Fishing for sand smelt requires a leader with a truly impressive conical sinker called a "jet balancer," and a three-pronged hook. Extreme caution is necessary when taking the hook out of its packet and tying it on, or the hook will immediately become hopelessly entangled in the line.

"You've got to take that thing off the right way, Pa!" Gaku said in a sharp voice as he watched me fumbling. "Even a first grader can do that! It's about time you learned to do it the right way so you can do it by yourself!"

I listened half amused and half shocked, and couldn't help thinking, This father-son relationship is absolutely, totally topsy-turvy! I indulged myself in thinking that this new aspect of our relationship was probably still limited to fishing, but I knew that as far as fishing went, I had been reduced in his mind to a pain-in-the-neck. My only real function, I suspected, was to take him places where he could fish.

The wind on the breakwater was blustery, and we didn't have much luck fishing for sand smelt. The only thing biting seemed to be wrasse and bluespotted boxfish. Before we knew it, it was past twelve and time for lunch.

We gathered our things together in a pile, and then I wrapped everything tightly in my parka and put several rocks on top so it wouldn't be blown away.

"Well, what should we have for lunch?" I asked, looking up at the clear but windblown sky. I scanned the anchorage in the harbor, and several of the buildings beyond it. On one of the buildings directly ahead I could see a sign that said, "Seafood Banquet Catering."

"How about some sashimi and hot rice?" I said.

"Sounds good to me," Gaku replied.

We started walking off the breakwater in single file, the short person leading the tall.

The wind was gusting so hard on top of the breakwater that Gaku stretched his arms out like wings on either side to keep his balance as he walked. Behind him and without his noticing, I thought of imitating him, but I felt too self-conscious, so I followed unsteadily, like the vertical tail fin of a careening airplane.

The first floor of the building I had noticed held a fish store, but there was a narrow stairway next to it. We climbed this to find a huge shop curtain draped above the doorway. It appeared to have been one of the banners that fishing boats flew as an invocation for a good catch; sure enough, the store even had a fishing boat's name, *Tokushin-maru*.

Two friendly and extremely garrulous middle-aged women were staffing the restaurant, and as soon as we entered they greeted us with a "Welcome, welcome! Why, thank you for coming! Here, why don't both you sit in the back where there's a good view of the ocean. Well, well, my goodness. . . ."

I had no idea what the "Well, well, my goodness . . ." part was all about, but without pausing in their chattering they set a table for the two of us with a view of the ocean.

The only other people in the restaurant were two local men, and a mysterious, depressed-looking, middle-aged couple. The two local men had apparently just finished eating and had some time on their hands, for they were reclining on the tatami mats, propping themselves up on their arms and watching a music show on the television that was on in the room.

One of the waitresses brought us tea and some salted squid, and with an ever-smiling face and a manner reminiscent of a fast-talking mouse said, "What would you like? Would you like to order right away? We've got lots of fresh fish today."

I scanned the menu. It had dishes of assorted sashimi ranging in price from two to ten thousand yen, and a wide variety of broiled fish.

"Feel pretty hungry?" I asked my four-meals-a-day son. With the waitress cordially smiling at him, he grinned back bashfully and managed a vigorous assent.

It was time to splurge. After all, I thought, the two of us wouldn't be able to eat together like this for over two months. I ordered an eight-thousand-yen fancy assortment of sashimi served on a dish shaped like a little wooden boat, some prawn sashimi, and tilefish marinated in saké lees. Then I asked the waitress to bring Gaku some rice right away, and some beer for me.

Alternately addressing Gaku and then me, the waitress said, "What a lucky boy you are, coming here fishing with your father. And did you come from Tokyo?"

I nodded, while Gaku smiled vaguely.

For lunch, the eight-thousand-yen sashimi dish proved to be truly deluxe. Tuna, sea bream, squid, abalone, turbot, and shrimp were all piled high in the middle of a little boat.

"Can I start eating?" Gaku asked, his eyes lighting up.

"Sure," I replied, "but it tastes better with rice."

"I know," he said. "Hey, look, this prawn's whiskers are still moving."

"That's 'cause it was still alive until a second ago," I said.

"Yumm," he said, as he began to eat pieces of his favorite sashimi in rapid succession.

My beer arrived, and a big bowl of rice was placed in front of Gaku. I started to drink the beer and sample the abalone sashimi. Its innards were surprisingly delicious. The mysterious depressed couple seated at the table next to us had their heads together and were discussing something in low voices. The restaurant phone rang, and one of the very voluble waitresses said something rapid-fire in the local dialect about the owner being out of sorts because a banquet scheduled for that night had been canceled.

"Pa, this tuna really tastes great," Gaku said, staring straight at me and looking so serious that I nearly burst out laughing. We had always had exactly the same appreciation of good food, and when he was smaller and we had tuna sashimi at home, we had some serious disputes over who was going to get the biggest portion.

"See?" I said. "Just like I always told you, tuna makes the best sashimi. But hey, don't hog all of it. Try some of this squid and shellfish, too."

"Naw, I'll let you have that, Pa," he said with a mischievous laugh.

I ordered my second bottle of beer, and then tried what was supposed to be a specialty of the house—squid innards marinated overnight. The broiled tilefish marinated in saké lees also arrived, and Gaku instantly began reaching for it.

"Hey, this stuff is great, too!" he exclaimed.

"Of course," I said. "Marinating something in saké lees usually makes it taste good. When I was in elementary school like you, my favorite box lunch was always marinated salmon." Outlining a box in the air with both hands, I said, "I used to take a square lunch box this big to school with me."

"No kidding," Gaku commented. He wasn't really very interested in what I was saying; he was too busy polishing off most of the tuna in the sashimi boat.

"Hey," I said. "How about leaving a little of that for me."

"Don't worry, Pa, I will," he said.

Outside the restaurant window we could see fishing boats coming in to anchor. The wind was apparently still blowing hard, for the little yellow banners they flew were fluttering crazily in the wind.

My second beer took effect much faster than usual, and from somewhere deep inside I felt the warmth of intoxication spread throughout my body. I began to feel terribly tender.

I only had three days left. In three more days I would be in Siberia. For the life of me, I could not imagine what it would be like in a world where the temperatures got down to minus fifty or sixty degrees centigrade.

"By the way," I suddenly said. Something had occurred to me, and I started to vocalize it without really considering what I was going to say. It was a surprising way to start a question, even for me. "By the way, Gaku," I continued, "what do you want to be when you grow up?"

He looked at me for a second, and said, "What?" It was, I realized, the first time I had ever asked him such a question.

"When I grow up?" he repeated, with an uninterested look.

"Yes."

"Hmm. Let's see," he said. Then in a low voice he added, "I think I'd like to be an adult."

"I'm serious," I said, using a somewhat stronger tone.

He appeared to sense what I was after, for he suddenly grinned as if to throw me off. Then, rubbing his shaved head with one hand in a self-conscious gesture, he said, "Well, gee, I like fishing, so if I could, I'd like a job catching fish."

I don't know why, but his reply seemed very funny, so I ended up grinning just like him and saying, "I see. So you'd like a job catching fish."

To most people, "a job catching fish" would mean a fisherman, but he hadn't said that. He was just being honest, and telling me how he honestly felt at that moment. He was my own son, and I might be biased, but I couldn't help suddenly thinking what a fine kid he was. I could tell I was beginning to feel the effects of the beer.

Our very talkative, mouselike, middle-aged waitress returned with some seaweed salad. "Everything fine?" she asked. "Does it taste okay?" Clearing off Gaku's now spotlessly cleaned rice and miso soup bowls, she added, "Sorry I brought your dishes in the wrong order."

I thought about the fact that a month after I returned from Siberia I was scheduled to leave on yet another trip—to an uninhabited island called Amchitka at the end of the Aleutian chain. It was to be another voyage of discovery, in which I would travel out of Alaska proper by airplane and helicopter along a virtually unexplored route. Later, in the summer, I was scheduled to spend a month crossing Siberia, and then after that I was supposed to travel across the Sahara Desert. I decided, in a rather expansive mood, that whenever I returned from a long trip in the future I would take my boy on an overnight fishing trip. I wasn't sure why I had suddenly thought of this or why I felt so good about it, but I knew that each time I returned from a trip he would have changed dramatically.

"Listen, Gaku," I said. "I'm leaving again in three days, but when I come back I'm going to take you fishing to Miyake Island, understand?"

"Umm, that sounds good," he said.

Commercial fishing seemed to be coming to an end for the day, for outside the restaurant window I saw two more boats straining against the wind as they slowly entered the harbor.

Since Gaku hadn't caught a single sand smelt in the morning, in the afternoon he moved to a spot under a tetrapod on the other side of the breakwater, changed his leader, and decided to target a different type of fish.

"I'm gonna go after some marbled rockfish with some drift lining," he said, his little nostrils flaring in anticipation.

The wind on the other side of the breakwater was gusting in great swirls, so I decided to continue fishing for sand smelt in the same spot as in the morning. Having nearly given up on actually catching anything, I also wanted to huddle in my parka and doze in the afternoon sun.

From where I sat I could see the lighthouse breakwater. Perhaps because the wind had died down somewhat, there was one man standing on it with a fishing rod. Directly in front of me, the sea had calmed down quite a bit, but when the wind rushed over its surface, it whipped it into patterns and made it look as if it had been turned inside out and was glowing white; the white area occasionally took the shape of a giant ellipse, which sped off to deeper waters.

I gave up watching my float, and with the sound of the wind roaring above my head, began thinking about the journey I was soon going to embark upon.

After thirty minutes of being lost in thought, three black fish were suddenly dangled in front of my eyes. They were all still alive and flapping vigorously, and my face was instantly covered with ocean spray. I instinctively dodged and yelled something silly like "Yow!" but then I heard Gaku yell from above me, "I got 'em, Pa! I got 'em." He had tied the fish to a chainlike device and lowered it down to me from the top of the breakwater.

"Don't scare me like that," I said.

"They're mighty fine fish, don't you think? They put up a good fight."

"Rockfish?"

"Yeah. They were hanging out at the bottom of the tetrapod. You ought to try it yourself. They really bit hard. I think if we try we can catch lots more."

"Really?"

"You wanna try?"

I really wanted to daydream a little longer, so I fibbed and said, "No, no thanks. I think I'll keep trying a little longer here for some sand smelt."

"If you want to try, Pa, I can rig your line for you real quick."

"Thanks," I said. I looked up. In his left hand he was holding his pole, and with his right hand he was brandishing the chain with the three rockfish—it seemed a magnificent, triumphal pose.

I had never seen the sort of chain to which he had tied the fish. It was specially designed so that several could be attached, and it had huge cliplike devices that could be run through the gills of each fish.

"What do you call that thing?" I asked.

"It's a stringer. You put it in the water, and the fish can keep swimming.

"No kidding." I stared at this terrifying gadget. I was impressed, both because he had employed such an incredible thing that I had never seen before, and because he was so absolutely absorbed in what he was doing. And at the same time I finally understood why, despite my repeated suggestions, he had resisted buying a creel at the tackle shop the day before. Gaku was already plunging way, way ahead into a world of which I knew nothing.

We stayed and fished until the last minute before our train left, and by then Gaku had caught twelve marbled rockfish.

Three days later I left on my trip to Siberia. Traveling in a grand, sideways-V-shaped course, I flew eleven hours from Narita airport to Moscow, then six hours on the domestic Soviet airline to the city of Yakutsk in eastern Siberia. In Yakutsk I entered a world that was already minus forty degrees centigrade. Upon leaving through the triple-layered doors of the airport terminal, I found the city shrouded in fog. The fog was thick, almost like cold milk, and it blanketed the city without letup from dawn to dusk; cars and people suddenly appeared like ghosts out of nowhere and then faded out of sight just as quickly. One local resident told me this fog was called "residential fog." He said the steam from cooking, the exhaust from automobiles, and the breath that people exhaled all froze instantly on contact with the minus-forty-degree air. Then all this floated along in the air, creating a fog that never lifted.

I had decided not to worry too much about my family on long trips overseas. If I started worrying about things, I knew there would be no end to it, and besides, I was in an area from which it was extremely difficult to telephone. If I resigned myself to my situation, I felt I would be better able to concentrate on the immediate reality before me.

Ten days after my little trip with Gaku to what now seemed "the lazily warm" Izu Peninsula, I entered the town of Oymyakon, the coldest spot on earth. The day I arrived it was minus fifty degrees centigrade. At eleven o'clock in the morning, a Siberian sun with the blurred contour of a half-boiled egg finally staggered over the horizon, rolled across a line of trees toward the west, and then was sucked under the horizon again at around two in the afternoon.

At the end of this three-hour "day," darkness took over. I normally drank vodka and went to sleep, but since this night seemed endless, I lay awake and began to ponder things. My little trip with Gaku to Izu already seemed like something that had happened years before, and the super-heated scenery of New Guinea where I had been only a few weeks ago seemed like an ancient memory. I knew Gaku would be starting his winter vacation. He had said that he and a couple of pals were going to Tomosuke Noda's place at Lake Kameyama to camp out—that they were going to pitch a tent, fish for black bass and crucian carp, and cook for themselves. Knowing this, on the day of my departure for Siberia I had left my own sleeping bag and a special camping headlamp on his bed for him. Lost in thought for what seemed an eternity, I wondered whether or not he had remembered to take them with him.

In the midst of the oppressive Siberian night, I thought about how my two-day present to Gaku had been a truly precious and wonderful time for me, too. Just thinking about it made me finally relax and feel at peace.

I rode on a sturdy Yakut pony at Oymyakon. It was fifty-nine degrees below zero centigrade—so cold that his face froze white, and when he drooled his saliva instantly froze into icicles that hung from his jaw. The horse was able to withstand the extreme cold, but I and the other members of my party quickly found that if we exposed our faces to the air too long they became swollen and dark red, and that unless we were careful we lost all feeling in our extremities. When we inhaled, we could hear the hair in our nostrils crackling as it froze; the few microns of watery fluid that normally covered our eyeballs also apparently began to freeze, for whenever we blinked we could feel a strange resistance on the surface of our eyes. In this frozen world of strange sights and sensations, I made absolutely sure that I kept moving.

The New Year had already begun when my four-week journey in the land of bitter cold ended. I arrived at Irkutsk, the largest city in Siberia, and there, from a room in a big hotel overlooking the Angara River, I called home for the first time. The phone lines in Siberia were apparently extremely limited, though, for I could not get a connection.

I wondered how the New Year holiday was going for Gaku and Noda at Lake Kameyama. It was still quite cold where I was, with the daily temperature in the minus forties.

Late at night on the eighth of January, my call finally went through.

"Everyone's fine," I heard my wife say, her voice sneaking out from between the crackling and hissing static. "Gaku came back from Noda's place yesterday, so the house is as noisy as usual again."

"Is he still awake?" I asked.

Apparently she couldn't hear me, for she kept saying in a shaky-sounding voice, "What? What did you just say?" Sometimes her voice was loud, and sometimes it was weak, and I feared that any second we might not be able to hear each other.

"Gaku!" I said in a loud voice. "Get Gaku!"

She seemed finally to understand, for way behind the popping static, I heard her say, "I'll get him right away." Then my receiver was filled with just static: she had apparently gone to get him. Listening to nothing but static gave me a surprisingly desolate feeling, and I began to worry what would happen if the line suddenly went dead. But shortly thereafter I heard Gaku, sounding like he was right next to my ear, say in his laid-back voice, "That you, Pa?" The snap, crackle, and pop of the static had suddenly decreased, and the signal had begun to come through much clearer.

"You okay?" I asked.

"Yeah. You okay, Pa?"

"I'm fine. I'll be back home for a while in a month."

"Oh," he said.

"Did you have a good time camping out at Noda's?"

"Yeah. It was lots of fun. But it was cold."

"Who'd you go with?"

"To-chan and Mi-chan and Kii-chan. There were four of us altogether. We stayed in a tent."

"I'll bet that was fun."

"Yeah. We played 'chicken.' We even cooked our meals by ourselves. But the curry we made was too spicy to really eat. I ate it anyway, though."

"How about the fishing?"

Next to Gaku's voice, I began to hear a low snapping and hissing, which sounded like a huge, terrifying animal.

"By the way," Gaku said, with a little laugh. "By the way, I fell in the sea."

"What? What sea?"

"Over at Kamogawa."

"You were fishing?"

"Yeah."

"You mean you fell off a breakwater? Were the waves big?"

"What? What did you say?"

We were again hit by a swirling wave of static, and our voices suddenly fluctuated on the line.

"The waves," I said. "The waves. Was there a lot of wind and waves?" I was impatient, and felt like he was falling off a breakwater into the sea right there and then. I clenched the receiver and raised my voice. And for a second, way on the other side of the restless static storm that was approaching, I imagined the white-capped, pounding surf Gaku and I had experienced on our trip to Izu, rising and sinking away.

"I'm talking about the waves and the wind! Did you get dragged by the current?"

"What'd you say? Waves?" Gaku's laid-back voice suddenly rose in volume, but so did the popping and hissing of the static, and it soon submerged him. I could barely hear something that "sounded" like him talking in the distance. I held my breath, and tried to listen as hard as I could. But the storm of interference intensified and in the darkness of the night, on top of what had been a hissing and snapping noise, I heard the swelling roar of what sounded like thousands of insects simultaneously beating their wings.

Then, like an arrow fired into the midst of this incredible static, I heard the voice of a Soviet woman, apparently an operator, saying, "Allo! Allo!"

Her voice, trembling slightly, wanted to end the connection that Gaku and I had. "Allo! Allo!" she said again.

I knew Gaku probably couldn't hear me, but I yelled straight into the raging static storm anyway: "Gaku, you numbskull! Don't fall in the ocean again, okay? Be careful!"

There was more snap, crackle, and hiss, and a sound that reminded me of a monster skating at incredible speed inside the phone line. It seemed to continue forever.

I thought perhaps that if I just waited patiently the connection might suddenly improve. I kept the receiver to my ear and repeated over and over, "Hey, Gaku! Can you hear me?"

A crazy-sounding woman's voice zigzagged through the line, repeating, "Allo! Allo! Allo!" A noise like tons of sand being blown into a pipe continued off and on for a while, and then I heard the popping and hissing of the static storm growing closer again.

I gave up. I put the phone down and sighed. The palm of the hand that had gripped the receiver was oozing sweat. I wiped my hand on my shirt, and turned off the light on the nightstand next to the phone. Then I slowly stretched out on top of the bed and lay there face up.

"That numbskull," I said to myself out loud, staring at the ceiling in the darkness. "Imagine, falling into the sea!"

Then, for some inexplicable reason, a silly feeling came over me; in a deliberately exaggerated fashion, with my body shaking on top of the bed, I laughed until I was utterly exhausted.

I left the Soviet Union on the flight that departs Moscow at exactly five in the evening. It is supposed to be the best flight to take because you can have a glass of whiskey and finish your evening meal, go to sleep early, and arrive in Japan the next morning. But for some reason I wasn't sleepy. It may have been because I had slept like a log the night before on the Siberian Railway from Leningrad to Moscow, but it was probably also because I had been away from home for two months and was a little excited.

The reading light on the Aeroflot plane was awfully dim, and after the cabin lights were turned out it was hard to see. The book I had was in small print, and after staring at it for a while I developed a heavy, painful feeling behind my eyes. This was extremely distressing, for I had wanted to read the book for nearly five years, and I had only gotten hold of it four days before.

While traveling across Siberia I had read nearly all the books I had brought with me from Japan, so by the time I arrived in

Leningrad I was suffering from fairly severe reading withdrawal symptoms. Tomosuke Noda, however, had sent me Alan Moorehead's *The White Nile* from Japan, addressed to my hotel. I had plunged hungrily into it with a deep sense of gratitude for his friendship, feeling relieved because it was laid out in two columns and set in dense eight-point type; I was certain it would last me for the four remaining days of my trip.

As luck would have it, after deliberately saving the most interesting parts of the book for the flight home, I could hardly read because of the poor light in the cabin. Damn Soviet planes! I silently cursed, and shut my eyes for a while. Then, with nothing better to do, I started staring out the window of the plane. I was seated just behind the wing, and in the weak light cast from inside the plane, I could just barely make out the CCCP letters inscribed on all Aeroflot planes. I had no idea what we were flying over, but judging from the time and our course, I guessed that we had crossed the Ural mountains and were over Siberia, somewhere along the coast of the Arctic Ocean.

In front of the wing, way off in the black distance, I saw a white light faintly glowing on the ground. When I squinted hard, I saw that it was a snaking, thin line, and I realized it was really a river flowing through Siberia, its surface frozen and dimly reflecting the light from the stars. Way, way beyond the river there were a few lonely lights clumped together and twinkling in the frigid air; they were probably frontier villages or outposts of fur trappers, scattered here and there on the permafrost ground. I thought about how, only a few days earlier, I myself had been traveling around this extremely cold land. I felt somehow terribly impressed, and at peace with myself. With my face pressed up against the window, I sipped my East German whiskey, feeling my throat tingle as it went down.

I stared at the frozen river below me in the darkness, and thought about the souvenirs I was bringing Gaku from Siberia.

In a general store near the Lena River, which flows from Eastern Siberia into the Arctic Ocean, I had bought him some Soviet-made fishing tackle and a hand-drill used for making holes in the ice. I had been especially taken by the drill, with its rustic, utterly utilitarian, Soviet design. The ice on the Lena was over a meter thick, but by vigorously cranking the drill one could open a hole fifteen centimeters in diameter in two or three minutes. When I got back to Japan, I thought, it would be fun to go with Gaku to one of the five lakes around Mt. Fuji while it was still winter and they were frozen over. We could use this extraordinarily powerful drill and bore hole after hole in the ice to fish for pond smelt.

With one thing and another, I had been away from home for nearly three and a half months, so I had also bought a giant brass frying pan for my wife and a reindeer skin for Tomosuke Noda. I had packed both the frying pan and the skin in my suitcase, but because the fishing tackle for Gaku looked as if it would bend or break under too much pressure, I had put it in my carry-on bag. I kept staring out the window and thinking, hoping I would fall asleep, but I never felt the least bit drowsy. Out of boredom I finally took the fishing tackle from my bag and spread it out on top of the foldaway table in front of my seat. In the dim light of the overhead reading lamp, there was something amusing about the roughly made Soviet lures and floats. I examined each one slowly and carefully, and spent an eternity wondering what Gaku would think when he saw them.

Just when I had finally managed to nod off for a couple of hours, it was dawn and we began to prepare for landing. Feeling disgruntled, I rubbed the sleep from my eyes and looked outside. The morning sky over Japan was a clear, pale blue that spread far into the distance. Below I could see the ground around Mt. Tsukuba covered in snow.

I finally arrived home. It had been frigid in Siberia, but it was also shockingly cold in the area around my home on the Musashino plain outside of Tokyo. As always, upon my return from long overseas trips, my wife had taken the day off and had a "real Japanese breakfast"—complete with piping hot rice, fermented natto soybeans, seaweed, Chinese cabbage pickles, and miso soup with green onions-waiting for me.

Knowing Gaku wouldn't be home until after two o'clock, when I finished eating I stretched out on the floor under the blankets of our little kotatsu heater-table and dozed off.

When I next came to, Gaku was standing right above me.

"Hey, Pa!" he said in his usual husky voice. "Time to wake up!" Without so much as a smile, he added, "Bring me anything?"

Having been awakened from a state of blissful slumber, I got up feeling less than overjoyed and led Gaku to my room, where I had his presents. On the way I sensed that something about him was different. And I knew what it was right away. His hair was different. He no longer had a shaved head but a longer, sporty-looking crew cut. And his voice was different, too. His voice had always been low for a boy, but now, every once in a while, it suddenly slipped into a funny high pitch, almost like a falsetto.

I took another good hard look at my son's face.

"Hey, Gaku," I said. "What happened to your voice?"

He didn't seem to understand what I meant right away, for he looked embarrassed, widened his eyes, and said, "Whaddya mean 'what happened'?" Nothing special."

"Don't you think there's something a little weird about it?" I said.

"Naw," he said, staring back at me in disbelief. "There's nothing weird about it."

As he spoke, he slipped in and out of a falsetto at least an octave higher than his normal voice. And I suddenly realized:

His voice is changing. Sure enough, that's exactly what was happening. His voice was changing before he even realized it himself.

As Gaku explained it, the hair on his shaved head had sprouted so luxuriantly in the few months of my absence that he had had no choice but to visit a barbershop. And the old lady who cut his hair there had simply taken matters into her own hands and given him the crew cut that I now beheld.

His hairstyle was different. His voice was a little different. And there was something a little different about his overall demeanor. Feeling a little flustered and bothered, I handed him his present of fishing tackle. "Listen, Gaku," I said, making a greater show of importance than was really necessary, "this is really unusual stuff. I bought it in a little town in a place called Siberia. There's probably nobody else in all of Japan with anything like this!"

He spread the tackle out in front of him and made a remark like, "No kidding. Looks kinda junky to me. Think they can really catch fish with this stuff?"

This did not make me feel any better, but it was true that the one spinner Gaku had happened to pick up was awfully crudely made; so crude, in fact, that if one of the battle-hardened fish from the streams of Japan spotted it, the fish would probably split its sides laughing.

After giving Gaku his presents, I went with him to his room and had him tell me about his winter vacation. He told me how he and his pals had camped out at Noda's place, and how he had fallen into the sea at Kamogawa in Chiba Prefecture. I laughed harder than I had in a long time.

Apparently the boys had gone to Kamogawa on their own while they were staying at Noda's, but they had run into a veteran angler there by the name of Mr. Kato who had helped them out a lot. Kato was an employee of the Japanese National Railways, and spent all his free time fishing.

"And Mr. Kato, see, he knows everything about fishing," Gaku said. "He showed us how to catch half beak clams, and we caught lots of 'em. Then we had him shred 'em into strips for us and we ate tons. They tasted fantastic! Mr. Kato knows at least a hundred times more than you about fishing, Pa. You've got to try harder, like him. . . ."

As Gaku talked about Mr. Kato, the look in his eyes reverted to that of the excited little boy I was so used to.

"Man, those half beaks taste great," he said, for extra effect. "Shredded half beak. That's the way to go."

I knew then that he would soon suggest that we head for Kamogawa the next time we went fishing. And I nearly burst out laughing, for sure enough he promptly said, "So when we go fishing in February, let's go to Kamogawa. If Mr. Kato shows you how, even you could catch some half beak, Pa. I know you'd have fun."

That night I called Tomosuke Noda's place to tell him I had returned, and to thank him for all his help. I mentioned that Gaku's voice was starting to change, and that his overall demeanor was changing, too, and that it was a strange feeling.

In response Noda started telling me about his kayak dog Gaku, and how amazed he had been when he had been away from his home in Chiba for a while and then returned. Gaku seemed to have suddenly grown, and in a doglike way his voice seemed to have changed, too; he seemed, overall, to be much more "adult." He no longer ran eagerly to greet him and beg for a walk. Whether dogs or humans, Noda said, at some point in their growth phase they suddenly turn into adults.

All this change in Gaku the kayak dog was hard for me to imagine. Before leaving on my trip to Australia, Noda had been telling me how Gaku always ran joyfully after him, that once the dog had been so busy looking at him that it forgot to look where it was going and fell into Lake Kameyama; in fact, that it had fallen in several times. Indeed, the Gaku I best remembered was a rather scatterbrained pup mournfully howling Aroof-Aroof on top of Noda's kayak as we paddled on Lake Biwa. I had trouble visualizing any other type of Gaku.

After calling Noda, I abruptly told my son that we should shave his head when he had his next haircut—that shaved head really looked much more masculine.

He listened to me, nodded in a vague sort of way, and said, "Yeah, but it's too soon for a hair cut. My hair's hardly grown at all."

It occurred to me then that he might be tired of a shaved head, and might even prefer a more grown-out sporty crew cut, but I wasn't sure. If it were true, I knew I had no business forcing him to shave his head.

One other thing about Gaku had changed. Valentine's Day came again two weeks after I returned from my trip, and as in the previous year, he received three little boxes of chocolates. I wasn't on hand at the time, so I don't know who brought them, but my wife seemed to have a fairly good idea. She said that he had not received a thing from Makie Ishihara that year. Apparently Makie had dumped him.

Ah, I thought, it's not always easy being a man.